THE TRUTH
MEGAN WOODS

ISBN# 978-1-998532-29-2

1. Christianity 2. Devotions 3. Holy Bible 4. Meditation

Printed in the United States of America
Published in the United States of America

www.aheliapublishing.org
support@aheliapublishing.org

Ahelia Publishing

There is a God who generously loves each of us with an everlasting, unquenchable love. He chose us to belong to Him before we ever took a breath, and He made a way for us to come to Him so that we could be with Him in a perfect paradise, long after time ceases to exist.

He has an enemy, the liar, the one who wants to be like Him: adored, worshipped, and bowed down to. But this enemy cannot win against the Almighty God. His fate has been sealed.

That enemy may harass us—God's children—but his defeat is already written.

His tool of choice? Lies and confusion. He used lies and confusion with Eve in the Garden of Eden and continues to use them against us today. But we are secure in the knowledge of God's victory.

We are not victims but victors in Christ Jesus.

Our power lies in knowing the truth, and that truth comes from the Word of God. This knowledge provides us with a comforting security, a shield against the enemy's lies and confusion. Our King gave us this book for our security, and we must know what it says, and precisely how to use it as the weapon for which it was intended.

Within these thirty devotions, you will find some of the powerful truths the Master gave and come to understand how to live in peace and walk in joy. The joy that comes from living in the truth, from knowing that we are loved and chosen by God, is a source of hope and courage in our daily lives.

... and that's the truth.

See what kind of love the Father has given to us,
that we should be called children of God ...

and so we are.

THE TRUTH IS ...

HE LOVES

See what kind of love the Father has given to us, that we should be called children of God; and so we are.

1 John 3:1

God loves you. This fact is understated and uncomplicated, yet we cannot grasp the power swaddled in those three little words.

This love of God is no ordinary thing that we can know by comparison to earthly experiences of love. It is not a feeling; it is unswayed by the breezes of life. It is a transforming kind of love, rescuing us from darkness and transplanting us into light, moving us from a wayward, hopeless existence of wandering, into His family. But not as a stranger, but as a chosen, adopted child which extends to us the unmerited privilege of being His sons and daughters.

This unearned, underserved, unwavering love gives us reason to pause and consider how great a love must be for One to call us children even while wayward and living in hostility against Him, as we choose darkness over light, sin over righteousness. It would make more sense, and we could comprehend it readily if the Scripture was directed toward righteous, perfect, unflawed people, but that is not the case, for none fit that description.

Now, to be adopted by a pauper, we would become paupers. We would have little to no inheritance, nothing to look forward to except a life of hardship, poverty and trouble. We find this easy to believe because we understand a pauper owns nothing so has nothing to give.

Receiving nothing is easy. It takes no special skills, and no earning or deserving is required to receive nothing. One need not even hold out their hand to grab onto nothing.

But being adopted by a king would afford us everything the king has. We become heirs of the king, joint heirs with the others in the family, and given the right to be a part of his kingdom, no longer strangers but family. It is not so easy to freely receive everything, to accept the fact that we need not earn or work for it, but this is the love the king has for us; it's based on who he is, not on who we are.

Now expand this even further to realize it's not an earthly king who has adopted us, but the King of kings. The One Sovereign King. It is He who has extended such an invitation to anyone who would receive it.

How can a mind fathom such a thing, except to experience it? To experience it, we must believe it is true and from that belief, simply accept it. Once inside the family, once the spiritual adoption has been sealed by our believing, we become the King's child.

God is that King!

As joint heirs with Jesus, we share His inheritance, glory, and relationship with the Father. What does a wise and loving father do with a child he loves? He delights in that child. He is proud of that one. He gives grace when required, mercy when needed, and discipline when necessary. The King opens His treasury to His children, protects them, provides for all their needs, and allows them special privileges not afforded to those outside of His family.

This is the kind of love the Father has given to us, so that we could be called His children, and so we are!

WHAT TRUTH DO I NOW KNOW ABOUT GOD?

God is gracious and always good. God loves me just as I am and forgives me when I am wrong.

Is this characteristic of God an internal truth for ME? _yS_

- Write this characteristic on a sticky note and place it where you'll see it daily. GOD LOVES ME.

- Read the following verses on God's love: Ephesians 3:18-19, Romans 5:8, 1 John 4:10.

- On the following page, write down the lies you've been told that have made you doubt God's love for you. Use these Scriptures to find the truth: write them down.

MY PRAYER

> Father, in You are the treasures of Heaven and all the blessings of eternity. You chose me to belong to You and be a part of Your family. That concept is wildly beyond my ability to understand, but I choose to believe it.
>
> Thank you for adopting me. Thank you for wanting me to belong to You. Show me where I have been believing lies and empower me to replace those lies with the truth. The truth is I am my Father's child. You love me as I am, and You, King of the kings, delight in me. Help me understand more of what this means and enable me to believe it completely.

The liar whispers:

Words of rejection and hate. Always
dividing and causing confusion.
The enemy is a liar.

BUT GOD SAYS:

He loves me and is always here for me.
God will always bring good things in
my life and will always accept me
just the way I am. God loves me
unconditionally and will forgive me
of my sin. I am made in his image
and I am his child.
He loves me for me and gives me
Grace each and every day.
I have new and abundant grace each
day that I wake up. I wake up because
of God's Grace.

HE IS GOOD (1)

Oh give thanks to the LORD, for he is good; for his steadfast love endures forever!

PART ONE: 1 Chronicles 16:34

God is good. Full stop. Nothing more needs to be added, for that is a complete sentence brimming with truth and the fullness of wisdom. Everything we ever need is found in those three words ... nine little letters ... God is good.

And yet, it seems somehow insufficient, not because of its structure or form but because we misunderstand it, or perhaps we don't have the capacity, as humans, to fully grasp its depth. In a world that is so un-good, it can be challenging to find something, let alone someone, who is good by the standard that God is good. However, God's goodness is not defined by the world's standards. It transcends our understanding and is not diminished by the un-goodness we experience. It is a goodness that is constant, unwavering, and beyond our comprehension.

Of course, none is good, at least if we measure good by God's scale—and the truth is, it is His scale that matters. So, we must ask, "What is good? Where do we get our understanding of such things?" and "How do we transform our limited understanding into a full measure of such?"

Every person learns about the big world from their small world. A child picks up the basic concepts of life in their first four years. If that child was blessed with gentle, kind, protective, and patient parents, the child will grow up to believe the world is such. That child will be secure and find it simple to believe God is good.

Contrarily, if a child is raised in a household of turmoil, disappointment, broken promises, and being made to feel like a burden, that child will view God in this way. This child will have more difficulties believing God is good, because he has not experienced good from his earthly father.

In the middle is a variety of childhood experiences: being abandoned by a parent, being overly controlled, not being controlled enough, having a lack of care, having too much care, and so on. For instance, a child who was constantly criticized and never felt good enough may struggle to believe that God loves them unconditionally. Furthermore, children learn how to be noticed by their parents or caregivers. Were they given praise for achieving good grades or winning championships? Did they feel their identity was somehow found in what they did rather than who they were? The varieties are endless.

One might wonder why this all matters when considering God to be good. The answer is equally simple and complicated.

We each learn to view God as we view our childhood. While one might easily accept the fact that God is good and that His faithfulness is everlasting, another will say, "He will only love me if I behave properly, or if I succeed, or if I am without fault."

The enemy has many opportunities to whisper lies because we live in an imperfect world, were raised by imperfect people, went to an imperfect school, and had imperfect friends. It can be challenging to believe that we have a God who is perfectly good at all times, eternally faithful, and who will never let us down, when that has not been our experience.

But God ... the good, good Father, is good. Our feelings are not a measuring stick which He must live up to. He is good, full stop.

WHAT TRUTH DO I NOW KNOW ABOUT GOD?

_____

_____

_____

_____

_____

Is this characteristic of God an internal truth for ME?_____

- Write this characteristic on a sticky note and place it where you'll see it daily. <u>GOD IS GOOD</u>.

- Read the following verses on God's goodness: Psalm 145:9, Psalm 23:6, Psalm 100:4-5.

- On the following page, write down the lies you've been told that have made you doubt God's goodness. Use these Scriptures to find the truth; write them down.

MY PRAYER

Heavenly Father, You are a good God. I know this because Your Word tells me so, and I choose to believe the words rather than my feelings. Sometimes, in a hard circumstance, I do find it hard to believe You are good, but I trust that You are.

Help me when I struggle to hold onto this truth; give me strength to believe it and to count on the fact that You are good, even when I may not see it. Father, open my eyes to see where I wrongly learned that I must earn Your goodness, and correct my thinking to know that You are good at all times and in all situations.

The liar whispers:

_____

_____

_____

_____

_____

BUT GOD SAYS:

_____

_____

_____

_____

_____

_____

_____

_____

_____

_____

_____

_____

_____

_____

HE IS GOOD (2)

Oh, taste and see that the LORD is good! Blessed is the man who takes refuge in him!

PART TWO: Psalm 34:8
PART TWO: Psalm 34:8

God is good, but the enemy heaps lie upon lie in our minds, reminding us how others have failed us and so will God, but we mustn't weigh God's good on the scales of human good. His goodness is not determined by the actions of anyone or by our experiences. Once we realize that God is above what we know, that He cannot be measured by human scales, and that He is the very essence of good, we can change our view and give thanks.

Give thanks, for *HE IS GOOD*.

This God, the One who knows you by name, who called you, rescued you, paid your debt, and waits to bring you to His kingdom to dwell forever, is good. His goodness is not a fluctuating concept but a constant, unchanging truth. Thanksgiving will flow from your heart once this realization sinks into your soul. He is sinless, untainted by the world, and unaffected by His enemy—our enemy—so His goodness has always been and will always be.

You can count on it.

His faithfulness is no less than His goodness. He is good BECAUSE His faithfulness exists for all time, and because His faithfulness eternally exists, He is good. So, faithfulness and goodness are inseparable. One cannot exist without the other, and perhaps they cannot be divided, saying this is good and that it is faithful. Perhaps they can only exist simultaneously.

14

The enemy would argue with that. He would whisper lies that God is good only when you behave a certain way, give something, or say something. He shouts that God is only good when we deserve it, which we never do, making God never good —at least not for us. The enemy would want you to believe that God is only faithful when you are faithful. But these are the lies of the enemy, and there is no truth in them. We must turn a deaf ear to the lies of the liar, and shut his words down.

This is one reason we spin our wheels, trying desperately to be good ourselves, so we can earn God's goodness. We give what we don't have, say yes when we should say no, and run around endlessly trying to buy what is not for sale.

God's goodness is free to all who believe. Just receive that truth and let it begin to dictate your choices. Rather than living from a place of trying to earn God's goodness, the truth sets one free to live from the place of knowing God's goodness depends on God and can be neither gained nor lost—only accepted.

The truth is that God is good, and God is faithful. These two truths have no beginning and no end. They work together simultaneously, and everything else comes from the foundation of this truth. You did nothing to earn them, and you can do nothing to reject them. It's a divine mystery, a beautiful paradox at which we can only marvel. His goodness and faithfulness, existing in perfect harmony, are a testament to His divine nature. All that is required of you, is to believe.

And that's the truth!

WHAT TRUTH DO I NOW KNOW ABOUT GOD?

_____

_____

_____

_____

_____

Is this characteristic of God an internal truth for ME?_____

- Write this characteristic on a sticky note and place it where you'll see it daily. <u>GOD'S GOODNESS IS FOR ME</u>.

- Read the following verses on God's goodness for you: Psalm 16:2, Psalm 23:1-5, Psalm 31:19.

- On the following page, write down the lies you've been told that have made you doubt God's goodness for you. Use these Scriptures to find the truth: write them down.

MY PRAYER

Lord, You are good. All the time and without fail, I can trust that You are good to me and You are for me. You cause things to work together for my good, and You can be trusted.

As I consider what is keeping me from fully grasping this truth, bring what You would to my attention so I can dismiss what I should no longer hold on to and be free to hold on to You. Work in my heart so I am unafraid to trust You and give me the courage to believe You will never let me down.

The liar whispers:

_____

_____

_____

_____

_____

BUT GOD SAYS:

_____

_____

_____

_____

_____

_____

_____

_____

_____

_____

_____

_____

_____

_____

Have I not commanded you? Be strong and courageous. Do not be frightened, and do not be dismayed, for the LORD your God is with you wherever you go."

Joshua 1:9

God is present. He is everywhere at all times, fully present with each of us continually. We cannot comprehend this in our limited understanding and finite minds, but the King is omnipresent. He misses nothing. Psalm 139:7-10 says, *Where can I go from your Spirit? Where can I flee from your presence? If I go up to the heavens, you are there; if I make my bed in the depths, you are there.*

In the beginning, as Adam and Eve hid in the garden, God presented Himself for their regular evening walk. When the two didn't show, God called, "Where are you?" He was not asking because He didn't already know the answer; He was asking for their sake, not His. He wanted them to look at where they were and think about why they were there.

He asks us, from time to time, "Where are you?" for the same reason. But no matter where we are, He is there too. This is a fundamental aspect of His nature since He transcends any limitations.

In times of joy, He is there, celebrating with us. In times of sorrow, His presence brings comfort. Isaiah 41:10 reassures us. *So do not fear, for I am with you; do not be dismayed, for I am your God.* This promise reminds us that we are never alone, even in our darkest moments.

When the Israelites were standing at the mouth of the sea with no means to cross, the Egyptian army was right behind them. Possibly, they could hear the horses tromping on the hard desert floor. Maybe the children tugged on their mamma's tunics, asking how they would get across.

However utterly terrifying, yet God instructs the leader, Joshua, not to be afraid. It seems like a big ask, but the Lord reminds Joshua that he is not alone; God is with him and will be with him wherever he goes.

When we grasp the magnitude of this truth, it changes everything. Are you in a crisis? God is there. Facing a giant? God is beside you, steadying you. Because He is everywhere, it means that while He is with you—beside you, holding you up—He is also behind you, shoring you up so nothing can attack from behind. He is also ahead of you, making the way forward, and He is at the end, making it all work together for your good.

When we live with the awareness of God's presence, it changes our perspective. We begin to see His hand at work in our lives, guiding and providing for us in ways we may not have noticed before. Recognizing God's ever-present nature can transform how we live our daily lives. Often, we categorize our lives, inviting God into specific areas while keeping others separate. However, God desires to be involved in every aspect of our lives, from the ordinary to the massive.

While knowing that God is ever-present is comforting, we are also called to be present with Him. In our fast-paced world, distractions are everywhere, making it easy to lose sight of God's presence.

The enemy would have us believe God has abandoned us, that He had something else to do, or we were too burdensome. Perhaps someone did abandon you in your life, but God never will. Maybe people were too busy and left you to do hard things alone, but God is not too busy.

Trust Him. There is never a burden you will carry alone; He will take it. There is no trial you will face by yourself; He will be with you, empowering you. No matter what you face on this earth, you will not be alone.

The King walks beside you.

WHAT TRUTH DO I NOW KNOW ABOUT GOD?

_____

_____

_____

_____

_____

Is this characteristic of God an internal truth for ME?_____

- Write this characteristic on a sticky note and place it where you'll see it daily. <u>GOD IS WITH ME</u>.

- Read the following verses on God's presence with you: Psalm 23:4, Deuteronomy 31:8, Isaiah 41:10.

- On the following page, write down the lies you've been told that have made you doubt that God is with you. Use these Scriptures to find the truth; write them down.

MY PRAYER

> Thank you for Your presence in my life. You have gone before me, standing guard behind me, ensuring I am safe in every direction. You are so good to me. Help my human mind understand heavenly truths. Open my understanding to know You always surround me and that I am never alone.
>
> Teach me to structure my life around this truth and to combat the lies of the liar, who tells me that I am not enough and that You will leave. Lord, help me to sense Your presence and to always keep it in the forefront of my mind.

The liar whispers:

BUT GOD SAYS:

HE DELIGHTS

He sent from on high, he took me; he drew me out of many waters. He rescued me from my strong enemy and from those who hated me, for they were too mighty for me. They confronted me in the day of my calamity, but the LORD was my support. He brought me out into a broad place; he rescued me, because he delighted in me.

Psalm 18:16-19

God never changes. He is the same yesterday, today, and forever. This truth allows us to look at our verse, and while we understand it was David who penned the words, it is as true for us today as it was for David then.

David was in dire need of rescuing. He was being pursued by one who wanted him dead, and without the protection of the Father, King Solomon would likely have overtaken David and taken his head.

You might not be in quite the same situation, but a need is a need. Whether running through the mountains looking for a cave in which to hide or dodging a bill collector because you simply don't have what they are demanding, God sees your need as clearly as He saw David's.

By our definition, a need is something a person must accomplish or cover without the means to do so. I heard of a young single mother who was experiencing extreme poverty. Her children were fed, but that was the extent of her abilities. And then, one day, they heard a loud crash outside their home.

Looking out, they found their old but reliable vehicle was leaning to one side, a tire had exploded, and something drastic had occurred. On closer inspection, the mom found a tie-rod had snapped in two.

Looking into the situation, she called her brother, who worked in the car industry. He assured her that they no longer made the part and that it would be a special order costing over $1500. That mother did not despair. She knew the Lord delighted in her and decided to trust Him.

She was in deep waters and couldn't swim. A disaster confronted her, but she counted on the Lord for His support as her provider, father, and King. He did not fail her, and He will not fail you.

Three weeks later, that mom received a phone call from her brother, who told her to "go pick up your van." Of course, she hadn't gotten the piece nor paid the mechanic for anything, so she began to protest as she thought it foolishness. Her brother repeated himself. "Trust me—go pick up your van."

She walked the few blocks to the mechanics, and there, as good as new, was her van. Bursting into tears, she called her brother back and asked how such a thing happened, expecting that he must have bought the piece and somehow had it installed.

But God ...

The story was re-told about a man entering her brother's shop to order something for his truck. In talking, the woman's brother mentioned how it's too bad that parts go out of production and become impossible to buy. The man asked what the needed part was, and to both the men's surprise, when he found out which part was needed for which vehicle, he choked on his words as he said, "I have that exact part in my truck in the parking lot. I cleaned out my garage this morning and was taking it to the dump. I'm sure glad I stopped here first."

But God ...

The piece was shipped to the mechanic, who installed it for $80. God had brought the woman into a wide open space and rescued her, not because she was particularly special, famous, incredibly righteous, or had worked it all out in her own power. God rescued her because He delighted in her.

And if He can do it for that one, He can do it for you.

Trust in the Lord with all your heart; He will bring you out into wide-open spaces. He will rescue you because He delights in you.

WHAT TRUTH DO I NOW KNOW ABOUT GOD?

_____

_____

_____

_____

_____

_____

Is this characteristic of God an internal truth for ME?_____

- Write this characteristic on a sticky note and place it where you'll see it daily. GOD DELIGHTS IN ME.

- Read the following verses on what God thinks of you: Jeremiah 29:11, Psalm 139:16-17, John 14:2-3.

- On the following page, write down the lies you've been told that have made you doubt God's thoughts of you. Use these Scriptures to find the truth: write them down.

MY PRAYER

Father, in this life, I face many needs, and I trust that every time I come to You, You will rescue me. Teach me to be patient while I wait, deepen my trust in You and help me believe that You hear my prayers and delight in me. Give me an assurance that I can hold in my soul and that You will always help me in my times of need.

Remind me when I am in deep waters that You are there, and I need to reach out to You. Let me not grow weary, but instead, call me to Yourself so that I can find rest in You as I remind myself that You delight in me.

The liar whispers:

BUT GOD SAYS:

"Blessed is the man who trusts in the LORD, whose trust is the LORD. He is like a tree planted by water, that sends out its roots by the stream, and does not fear when heat comes, for its leaves remain green, and is not anxious in the year of drought, for it does not cease to bear fruit."

Jeremiah 17:7-8

What does trusting in the Lord look like practically? How does one live a life based on such a tall order? It's a common phrase among Believers. We've all said the words to a friend in crisis when we don't have the answer, and likewise, it's been repeated to us when we find ourselves in a tight place without a way of escape.

Trusting in the Lord brings a sense of security. It's not just a phrase; it's a promise. Those who trust in the Lord *will* be strong in hardship and fruitful even when there's been no rain. One who trusts in the Lord is steady. They are immovable.

We must realize that we surrender our desires when we trust the Lord. We set down what we want, the path we carefully forged out for ourselves, and stop scurrying around trying to make our lives look like the ones we've set up in our hearts. We surrender our way and say, "Lord, have Your way. I trust You know better than I."

It may seem safer to trust in our own abilities, but this is limiting because we are mere mortals. Our vision is confined to the present, but God's vision is all-encompassing. We have ourselves and a few others in mind, but God has eternity in His sight. Our impatience can lead to mistakes, hesitation when action is needed, and action when we should pause. But God is patient. He is never in a rush. He leads with gentleness and fills our souls with peace.

The Bible says *He works all things together for good* (Romans 8:28), but it never promises that there will be no hardships or trials along the way.

Trusting the Lord does not mean our path will be without hardship. However, life brings them whether we trust God or only trust ourselves. This is the reality of life. But if we trust the Lord, He will make the path straight. He will do what is best because He alone knows what that is.

Trusting Him will strengthen you, build you into a mighty warrior, and not lead you down a dead-end path. He knows the plans He has for us because He planned them.

But the liar would have you throw in the towel at the first sharp corner. At the slightest trial, the enemy will lie to convince us that God is not on our side and that He cannot be trusted. The liar will use fear, saying, "He will let you fail, He's left you, You are a disaster, You'll never get there."

The lies will continue, but a person who trusts in God can never be shaken. The one who trusts in the Lord will bear much fruit, and the enemy hates good fruit. He will work overtime to tempt you to trade your fruit for fear.

The King of Heaven will never let you down. Not everything will go the way you planned, or it might take years when you were hoping for months. But put your trust in the Lord, become unshakeable, steadfast, immovable. In this person, there is no fear; there is no doubt. And through this person, the Lord can move mountains.

As we learn to be steadfast in trusting the Lord, He will bring blessing after blessing. With each step, He blesses. As we surrender ourselves to Him, He blesses. The deeper we trust, the richer the blessings flow.

God never misses an opportunity to bless His children; let us never forget to notice them and be thankful for His goodness. If we make it a habit of counting His blessings, we will forget to wallow in our trials.

WHAT TRUTH DO I NOW KNOW ABOUT GOD?

_____

_____

_____

_____

_____

_____

Is this characteristic of God an internal truth for ME?_____

- Write this characteristic on a sticky note and place it where you'll see it daily. <u>GOD BLESSES ME</u>.

- Read the following verses on God's blessings for you: James 1:17, Numbers 6:24-26, 3 John 1:2.

- On the following page, write down the lies you've been told that have made you doubt God's blessings for you. Use these Scriptures to find the truth: write them down.

MY PRAYER

Lord, You bless me. When I count my blessings, I cannot name them all. You have been so good to me even when I have not recognized it. You take my struggles and turn them into successes. You are there when I feel alone and remind me that You surround me. Help me to trust You.

I trust You today, but give me courage on the days I don't, and remind me to begin counting my blessings again, for there is no end to them. Thank you for choosing me, giving me strength when I am weak, and courage when I am afraid.

The liar whispers:

BUT GOD SAYS:

HE IS THE LIVING WORD

"The word is near you, in your mouth and in your heart" because, if you confess with your mouth that Jesus is Lord and believe in your heart that God raised him from the dead, you will be saved. For with the heart one believes and is justified, and with the mouth one confesses and is saved.

Romans 10:8-10

Words possess a profound influence. They can either create or destroy. As Proverbs 18:21 states, *the tongue wields the power of life and death*, and we live out the consequences of our speech. This is why I hold music in high regard. It provides a platform to echo worshipful, truthful words, embedding them in our hearts and minds. Words serve as a compass, guiding us toward truth. David understood this in Psalm 42:5, when he preached to his own soul, *Why are you in despair, my soul? And why are you restless within me? Wait for God, for I will again praise Him.*

David heard his words. His soul listened to his reprimand and the reminder to wait for God. From his example, we can learn that our souls (mind, will, and emotion) hear our words and respond.

In psychology, there is a term known as *catharsis*. It refers to purging one's mind of what is troubling it by talking the situation through, releasing the burden from one's soul. The soul hears what comes out of our mouths, and we act per what our soul believes. It's a cyclical idea whereby what is in one's heart comes out through words. The soul hears the words and triggers the mind, will, and emotions to respond accordingly, confirming our beliefs.

If we walk in the fruit of our words, what must our words become? We already see that our personal salvation results from our spoken words and believing hearts (cyclical), so what else might we use our words for?

This is why the enemy works overtime, inserting his lies into our thoughts. He also knows the power of our words and wants us to speak wrong words.

He wants us to speak those lies out loud! When our soul hears lies, it responds accordingly and begins to act as though the lies are true. The lies might say, "Nothing ever works out for you; you should just give up," and so, the heart begins to believe that, and you might say no to opportunities that would be amazing. If you believe nothing ever works out for you, why bother trying?

However, if you take those lies and use God's Word against them, speaking the truth of Scripture instead, two things will happen over time. First, the lies will quiet down and eventually stop entirely; second, you will begin to find success in the avenue you pursue. According to Proverbs 18:21, *we will walk in the fruit of your tongue.*

The truth is that we all walk in the fruit of our tongue, whether sweet or sour. If we constantly walk around saying, "I'm such a loser; I never do anything right," we will live in that fruit: sour, rotten, stinking fruit.

However, if we change those words to align with the powerful truth of the Scripture, such as, "I can do all things through the strength of Christ Jesus. Even if it's difficult, the Lord will give me strength." Or, "The Lord will bless me coming in and going out. He is my rock, my fortress, and I trust Him," we will quickly begin to notice the lies fade, the fruit will become sweet and delicious, and we will see life begin to change.

It's not easy to change our words, but if we believe in the Word of God, He will help give us the rules: The power of life and death is in the tongue. To change our lives, we must change our words to match what God says and stop speaking the lies the enemy whispers because, as we've seen, our souls will hear and believe our words.

Words matter—choose yours wisely!

WHAT TRUTH DO I NOW KNOW ABOUT GOD?

_____

_____

_____

_____

_____

Is this characteristic of God an internal truth for ME?_____

- Write this characteristic on a sticky note and place it where you'll see it daily. <u>WORDS MATTER</u>.

- Read the following verses on the power of words: Psalm 19:14, Proverbs 10:19, Proverbs 16:24, Eph. 4:29.

- On the following page, write down the lies you've been speaking over yourself. Then, write down godly words that you can begin speaking about yourself and others.

MY PRAYER

You are the Living Word and have instructed us in Your Word to be aware of the power of the tongue. By confessing You are Lord, I have been saved. There is nothing I can do to make You cast me away, but You say that if I believe in my heart and speak it with my mouth, I am saved! How amazing You are, Father.

Bring to my mind an awareness of my words; when I say negative things about myself and others, highlight them so I can hear them and change my words. Father, You don't make junk, so remind me who I am in You and help me begin speaking those things. I want to live in good fruit.

The liar whispers:

_____

_____

_____

_____

BUT GOD SAYS:

_____

_____

_____

_____

_____

_____

_____

_____

_____

_____

_____

_____

_____

HE GIVES REST

Come to me, all who labor and are heavy laden, and I will give you rest.

Matthew 11:28

What's got you weighed down today? Are you carrying burdens that weigh on your soul, dragging you down and causing you to feel overwhelmed and exhausted? Burdens can do that. Take heart; there is rest for your weary soul. But there is a catch: you must be willing to lay down the burdens and not pick them up again. You must believe that the King will take care of you and make a trade with you: His rest for your burden.

We could all nod and think what a good trade this would be. We would extend our hands and say, "Here ya go, God. Take it all." But it's not so easy.

It takes trusting Him and believing He will take care of your burdens and all that is wearing you out. It takes giving up the desire to micro-manage the Master and leaving all you gave to Him with Him. Our natural instinct is to take them back. This is doubt. He doesn't operate in doubt. He operates when we trust Him.

God will never force us into action. He is a gentleman, and Matthew 11:29 reminds us, *He is gentle and humble in heart*. He knows what we need to be at rest, but He is gracious, telling us that answer and then leaving the decision to accept the answer up to us.

He has given us the guidebook to a rest-filled, peaceful life, but as with any guidebook, we must know what it says. One would be foolish to set to building a house without carefully examining the blueprints. The more lavish the home, the more detailed the building plans. No builder would take those plans and, never opening them, set them aside to collect dust.

It would take no time before the builder looked for those blueprints. After the third major problem, he would demand that those blueprints be studied carefully.

Yet, this is often how we live. We try to build our lives without knowing the blueprint. We cause ourselves (and others) so much anxiety, piling burden upon burden, wearing ourselves ragged. We scurry around trying to find solutions to problems when we have been given the answers! We have the blueprint. By studying it, we empower ourselves with knowledge and understanding and can live a life free from unnecessary burdens.

In studying the instructions, we will find a common theme from beginning to end: Trust the Lord. Just believe! This is what is required for the saving of our souls, to become children of God, to enter Heaven, and to receive anything from the Lord. This is what is required to live peacefully in the rest only He can give in return for our burdens.

The enemy wants you to believe that you have to micro-manage the Father. He will lie and make you wonder if God can be trusted or if you need to take care of yourself. But don't buy into those lies; they only produce more exhaustion, burdens, doubt, and trouble.

The truth will set you free!

What an exchange! Our burdens for His rest. Our anxieties for His peace. He is the great builder and will do what you cannot. Allow Him to build your house, and all who will dwell therein will lay down in peace and find rest for their weary souls.

WHAT TRUTH DO I NOW KNOW ABOUT GOD?

_____

_____

_____

_____

_____

_____

Is this characteristic of God an internal truth for ME?_____

- Write this characteristic on a sticky note and place it where you'll see it daily. <u>GOD GIVES ME REST</u>.

- Read the following verses on God's rest: Psalm 4:8, Isaiah 26:3, Exodus 33:14.

- On the following page, write down the lies you've been told that have made you think you don't deserve God's rest and that you need to earn it. Use these Scriptures to find the truth; write them down.

MY PRAYER

Father, I am tired. I have long tried to keep my boat afloat, even though it is full of holes! Provide me the courage to set my burdens at Your feet and the strength to leave them there! I don't want them back, and I don't want to tell You what to do with them. When I start to, please remind me that You are capable and don't need my help.

Help me to believe You have my life handled. Open my ears to listen to Your voice and show me what I need to learn in Scripture. Open my understanding and give me a strong desire for the truth found in Your Word.

The liar whispers:

_____

_____

_____

_____

_____

BUT GOD SAYS:

_____

_____

_____

_____

_____

_____

_____

_____

_____

_____

_____

_____

_____

_____

_____

HE PROTECTS

He will cover you with his pinions, and under his wings you will find refuge; his faithfulness is a shield and buckler.

Psalm 91:4

The world is troublesome. It seems there are new tragedies weekly, and we don't know where to run. Perhaps you feel like you don't belong here, in this world, but take heart; God has you here for a reason and a season.

Regardless of what might be going on in your life, how hard the struggle is, or how deep the wounds are, you can take refuge under His wing and find solace near the Master.

Looking back through the telescope of time, we see that in Jesus' day, there were problems. We can go back to His beginning when the enemy wanted Him dead and made a law stating that EVERY Jewish baby boy under a certain age was to be put to death. The king would catch Jesus in his trap by implementing a law of death. But God said no. He intervened so when the time came for those babies to be gathered, the King of kings, wrapped in swaddling clothes, was nowhere to be found.

What is so interesting about this Scripture is that God always does the doing. He will cover you. You don't need to run around looking for His pinions, looking to be covered. Look up—HE has already covered YOU. It's HIS job to cover and your job to take refuge.

If you were in the mountains and a storm was coming, you might run around looking for a cave or a giant tree to take shelter. You might find something reasonably secure and hunch beneath it, finding it has holes, and you are getting the wind and the rain beating you in the face. You dart out, looking for a better shelter. Finally, you find something to keep you safe and settle in for the storm's duration.

From your shelter, you can see the winds ravaging the forest, but you are untouched because of your shelter. You see the wind, but the wind does not see you. Your hair is blown because the wind got you while you scurried. While untouched now, in the search for shelter, you were windblown.

Likewise, the rains pelt everything around you; the ground becomes a pool, and the sky is dark. But you are dry because you found shelter. You see the rain, but the rain does not see you. You might be dripping wet because it was in the rain you searched for shelter. So while it can't get you now, hidden there in the shelter, it got you then while you were searching.

But God is the shelter. He is the covering in storms, and He finds you! All you need to do is take the shelter provided and watch, untouched, by the storm.

The enemy would have you believe the storm will take you out. He whispers, "You'll drown in this storm; nobody will help you. Nobody even cares that you are in this storm." If you listen to the lies, fear will settle in, and you will begin scurrying to find shelter. Anxiety will grip you, and the storm will pummel you. The evil one will try to convince you that finding shelter is up to you and stopping the storm is your responsibility, but those are mere lies of the enemy. The lies can be ignored if you know the truth.

Peace is found when you keep your eyes not on the power of the storm but on the strength of the shelter. The truth is that God is your shelter; you have no need to scurry to find Him—just look up. He is already covering you. His faithfulness is a wall protecting you. You are secure under the wings of the Master; safety is always found.

Storms will come in this world because evil does dwell here. But the Sovereign Lord, King over all, will keep you under the shelter of His wings. He will guard you and say, "I know, child, you can see the storm, and it is scaring you, but do not worry. I've got you covered."

WHAT TRUTH DO I NOW KNOW ABOUT GOD?

_____
_____
_____
_____
_____
_____

Is this characteristic of God an internal truth for ME?_____

- Write this characteristic on a sticky note and place it where you'll see it daily. <u>GOD PROTECTS ME</u>.

- Read the following verses on God's protection over you: Isaiah 54:17, Psalm 46:1, 2 Thessalonians 3:3.

- On the following page, write down the lies you've been told that have made you doubt God's protection. Use these Scriptures to find the truth: write them down.

MY PRAYER

There seem to be so many storms swirling around me, and while I don't have the answers, I trust in You to shelter me. Lord, keep me safe while I navigate this world; open my eyes to see which way You would have me to go; open my ears to hear Your voice and help me when I am afraid, to trust in You.

Help me tune out the voice of the liar, who tries to tear me up and remind me daily that I can live in peace when I take my eyes off the storm and recognize the security of the shelter.

The liar whispers:

_____

_____

_____

_____

_____

BUT GOD SAYS:

_____

_____

_____

_____

_____

_____

_____

_____

_____

_____

_____

_____

_____

_____

HE IS THE ROCK

The LORD is my rock and my fortress and my deliverer, my God, my rock, in whom I take refuge, my shield, and the horn of my salvation, my stronghold.

Psalm 18:2

None of us get through life without seeing a few hard days; they are just part of the journey. But difficulties are never without purpose. Whether we believe that the Lord sends trials or not, He allows them to touch each of us occasionally. Some trials are small and last momentarily; others are too heavy to carry and threaten to make us crumble under their weight.

Amid life's trials, we seek stability and reassurance that all will be well and we will make it. We want to know we won't buckle under the weight of the burden and someone will come along and take it from our shoulders.

This is when we are reminded of God's role as our Rock. Just as rock provides a solid base to build upon, God offers the steadfast support we need to bear up under life's storms. When winds of adversity howl and waves of uncertainty crash around us, we can stand firm on the unshakeable foundation of His faithfulness; we can stand on the Rock.

Recognizing God as our Rock means acknowledging our needs and limitations. Only when we reach the end of ourselves can we grab onto the Rock. We must empty our hands and cling tightly to Him.

God's strength is most evident in our vulnerability. When we lean on Him, we discover that our weaknesses become the platforms through which His power operates. Instead of striving to be self-sufficient, we are called to surrender our burdens to the One who can carry them. They are not too heavy for Him. This means that when we feel weak, we can turn to God for strength, and He will empower us to overcome our challenges.

Of course, the enemy will try to convince you that the Rock cannot be trusted and nobody will help you. He will work to cause us to try and find solutions or to drag the heavy weight behind us, like a chain holding us back. Don't believe those lies.

God is our Rock, and He can certainly be trusted to carry what we cannot and to be our sure foundation when our lives seem to be shaking all around us.

To fully experience God as our Rock, we must build our lives upon Him rather than run to Him only when life throws us a curveball. This means living in obedience to His Word, trusting in His promises, and seeking His guidance in all aspects of our lives.

Jesus, in the Sermon on the Mount, illustrates in Matthew 7:24-25: *Therefore everyone who hears these words of mine and puts them into practice is like a wise man who built his house on the rock.* It is not enough to acknowledge His strength; we must also live in obedience to the Word. Each act of faith, every prayer, and every moment spent in His presence reinforces our spiritual foundation.

As we navigate the days of life, aware that some will be heavy, we can be confident that He is our Rock—our source of strength, refuge, and constant companion. In moments of trouble, turn to Him and cling to the Rock, discovering peace and unwavering stability in His kindness and grace.

When we build our lives upon this unshakeable foundation, trusting God as our Rock, we can face any storm that comes our way.

WHAT TRUTH DO I NOW KNOW ABOUT GOD?

‚

Is this characteristic of God an internal truth for ME?_____

- Write this characteristic on a sticky note and place it where you'll see it daily. <u>GOD IS MY ROCK</u>.

- Read the following verses on God being your rock: I Samuel 2:2, Psalm 18:31, Psalm 62:2.

- On the following page, write down the lies you've been told that have made you doubt God's unshakeable strength and that He is your fortress. Use these Scriptures to find the truth: write them down.

MY PRAYER

God, You are my rock, and I desire to cling to You more daily. When I face trouble, lead me to the rock. When I am blessed, lead me to the rock. In all things, at all times, I want to cling to You, Lord. As I build my life in this world, I want to build on the rock, but when I forget and move to the shifty sand, call me back; never let me stay there too long, Lord.

You have blessed me with this life, and I thank You for all You do each day for me. I am sorry that even though You have done so much, I forget and run back to the sand. Keep my eyes on You, keep my hands free from sin, and keep my feet on the rock—that is You.

The liar whispers:

_____

_____

_____

_____

_____

BUT GOD SAYS:

_____

_____

_____

_____

_____

_____

_____

_____

_____

_____

_____

_____

_____

_____

_____

HE IS HOPE

... having the eyes of your hearts enlightened, that you may know what is the hope to which he has called you, what are the riches of his glorious inheritance in the saints, and what is the immeasurable greatness of his power toward us who believe, according to the working of his great might.

Ephesians 1:18-19

In this world overshadowed by uncertainty, hope can be hard to find. It is essential to the human experience, for without hope, what does one have? Hopelessness feels heavy, like a wet blanket has been thrown over us, extinguishing the spark we once had. Without hope, one sees no point in continuing in their ventures.

Hope fuels our aspirations, comforts us in times of distress, and motivates us to persevere. Romans 15:13 says, *May the God of hope fill you with all joy and peace as you trust in him, so that you may overflow with hope by the power of the Holy Spirit*. We are reminded that hope is not merely a human endeavor but a divine gift. As the source of hope, God desires to fill our hearts with joy and peace, enabling us to overflow with hope in every circumstance. Hope leads to perseverance and tenacity to keep on going, pressing through all that might threaten to stand in the way.

Life can sometimes be overwhelming; we may feel like we are drowning in despair. Whether it's personal struggles, relational conflicts, or political crises, these challenges can dampen our sense of hope. Yet, during these same moments, God invites us to draw closer to Him. Psalm 42:11 encourages us, saying, *Why, my soul, are you downcast? Why so disturbed within me? Put your hope in God, for I will yet praise him, my Savior and my God*. This verse serves as a powerful reminder to redirect our focus from our troubles to God Himself. Even in the depths of despair, we can choose to place our hope in the One who is faithful and unchanging.

The enemy tries to convince us that we are without hope.

He understands the devestation hopelessness can have on the human soul and so, he lies, whispering that we have no hope in this life, and not to go to God for hope, because He will let us down. These are lies that we dare not believe even for a second.

The hope we have in God is anchored in His promises. Throughout Scripture, we see God's unwavering faithfulness. In Jeremiah 29:11, God declares, *For I know the plans I have for you, plans to prosper you and not to harm you, plans to give you hope and a future.* This promise reassures us that God has a purpose for our lives, even when we cannot see it. Our circumstances may seem bleak, but God's plans extend beyond our understanding. He is working all things together for our good, and this truth instills hope within us.

James 1:2-4 reminds us to *consider it pure joy, my brothers and sisters, whenever you face trials of many kinds.* At first, this may seem counterintuitive. How can we find joy in trials? The answer lies in the transformative power of hope. When we endure difficulties, our faith is refined, and we become resilient, inspired by the hope that God's presence brings. God uses trials to deepen our character and strengthen our hope. Romans 5:3-5 adds, *We also glory in our sufferings, because we know that suffering produces perseverance; perseverance, character; and character, hope.* As we navigate challenges, we are reminded that hope is not the absence of trouble but the assurance that God is with us.

Our ultimate hope as Believers is found in Jesus Christ. He embodies hope, having conquered sin and death through His resurrection. In 1 Peter 1:3, we read, *Praise be to the God and Father of our Lord Jesus Christ! In his great mercy, he has given us new birth into a living hope through the resurrection of Jesus Christ from the dead.* This living hope is not a distant dream but a present reality that transforms our lives, instilling in us a deep sense of confidence. Because Christ lives, we can confidently face tomorrow, knowing that our future is secure in Him.

WHAT TRUTH DO I NOW KNOW ABOUT GOD?

_____

_____

_____

_____

_____

_____

Is this characteristic of God an internal truth for ME?_____

- Write this characteristic on a sticky note and place it where you'll see it daily. <u>GOD IS MY HOPE</u>.

- Read the following verses on having hope in God: Jeremiah 29:11, Micah 7:7, Romans 15:13.

- On the following page, write down the lies you've been told that have made you lose hope in God. Use these Scriptures to find the truth: write them down.

MY PRAYER

God, hope is hard to find these days. There are so many things going on in the world and in my life that hopelessness is heavy on some days. But You promised to be my hope. You say You have plans for me, to give me hope and a future. I am unsure what my future looks like, but help me trust that Your perfect plan for me has worked out. You have aligned the details, and I only need to keep going.

Give me the courage to keep walking, even when I cannot see, and the strength to trust when I am afraid. Father, thank you for supplying hope; without You, there would be none.

The liar whispers:

BUT GOD SAYS:

HE IS WISDOM

If any of you lacks wisdom, let him ask God, who gives generously to all without reproach, and it will be given him.

James 1:5

In a world flooded with opinions and information overload, the quest for true wisdom is critical. Voices come from everywhere, telling us the *right* thing to do. But wisdom transcends mere knowledge; it is the ability to apply knowledge rightly and discern what is good and just.

As Believers, we know God is wisdom and recognize He is the ultimate source of all understanding, guidance, and insight.

The Bible frequently addresses the nature of God's wisdom. In Proverbs 3:19-20, we read, *The Lord by wisdom founded the earth; by understanding, He established the heavens.* This passage reminds us that the very fabric of creation is woven with divine wisdom. God's wisdom is not only foundational; it is also sustaining. Everything operates under His understanding, from the intricate balance of ecosystems to the complexities of human relationships.

God's wisdom is unsearchable and unparalleled. Romans 11:33 proclaims, *Oh, the depth of the riches of the wisdom and knowledge of God! How unsearchable his judgments and his paths beyond tracing out!* Unlike human wisdom, which can be flawed and limited, God's wisdom is perfect and eternal. When we seek wisdom, we are ultimately seeking God's heart and mind.

We are reminded in James 1:5, *If any of you lacks wisdom, you should ask God, who gives generously to all without finding fault.* This verse presents a captivating invitation: we can approach God with our questions and uncertainties. We often face decisions that require discernment—whether in relationships, careers, or moral dilemmas. In these moments, we must turn our hearts to God, asking for His guidance.

DAY TWELVE

Seeking God's wisdom involves more than mere inquiry; it requires humility and a willingness to listen. Proverbs 2:6 states, *For the Lord gives wisdom; from his mouth come knowledge and understanding.* When we earnestly seek God, we open ourselves to receive the wisdom He imparts. This wisdom is often revealed through prayer, Scripture, and the counsel of wise mentors in our lives.

Of course, the enemy would have us believe we don't need God, that we can look to the world for wisdom, and figure things out on our own. But 1 Corinthians 3:19 reminds us, *For the wisdom of this world is foolishness in God's sight.* Human reasoning can lead us astray, particularly when prioritizing self-interest over righteousness. We see this in society's many pitfalls—moral relativism, greed, and pride—where human wisdom fails to provide the clarity we need. Worldly wisdom often leads us in the wrong direction away from God, saying God is no longer required in the world and that only fools follow Him.

But as Believers, we are called to discern between worldly wisdom and God's wisdom. This discernment often requires us to challenge societal norms and seek a higher standard. Colossians 2:3 states, *In whom are hidden all the treasures of wisdom and knowledge.* Finding wisdom in Christ means aligning our thoughts and actions with His teachings and recognizing that true wisdom leads to life, peace, and fulfillment.

When we embrace God as our source of wisdom, we begin to see the fruits of that wisdom manifest in our lives. Proverbs 2:10-11 says, *For wisdom will enter your heart, and knowledge will be pleasant to your soul. Discretion will protect you, and understanding will guard you.*

The wisdom of God not only enriches our understanding but also shapes our character and actions.

As we face uncertainties and questions, we know where the source of wisdom lies. By faith, and without doubt, we can go to the Father who gives graciously and abundantly and simply ask. He will answer every time.

WHAT TRUTH DO I NOW KNOW ABOUT GOD?

_____

_____

_____

_____

_____

_____

Is this characteristic of God an internal truth for ME?_____

- Write this characteristic on a sticky note and place it where you'll see it daily. <u>GOD GIVES ME WISDOM</u>.

- Read the following verses on God's wisdom: Ephesians 1:16-17, James 3:17.

- On the following page, write down the lies you've been told that have made you doubt that God will give you wisdom. Use these Scriptures to find the truth: write them down.

MY PRAYER

> You know, Father, even more than I do, that I need wisdom. In Your Word, You tell me that You will give me a generous portion of wisdom, and I need that today and every day. The world is tough to navigate, and it is difficult to know what is true, what is propaganda, and what is outright lies. I need wisdom from You to know how to walk the road set before me today.
>
> Don't let me go, Lord. Keep me near You and dependent upon You, for You are the one who holds every answer I need. Remind me every morning as I rise that You are the wisdom I require, and help me to believe and not doubt that You will supply every drop of wisdom I need.

The liar whispers:

BUT GOD SAYS:

53

... do not be anxious about anything, but in everything by prayer and supplication with thanksgiving let your requests be made known to God. And the peace of God, which surpasses all understanding, will guard your hearts and your minds in Christ Jesus.

Philippians 4:6-7

This Scripture is swelling with wisdom on living a life steeped in peace, even in a world without peace. Such a thing is only achievable when one lives in alignment with the teachings of our Heavenly Father. Even then, one cannot fully understand it; it is too wild for our limited understanding. We do not need to understand it to walk in it.

There is much to be anxious about in one's life, and it seems too much for the Lord to suggest otherwise. In fact, today, the list might seem endless with temptations to be anxious. This Scripture suggests the things we are bringing the Lord are enormous, for small things don't require pleading and, as some versions say, petitioning.

Yet the Word of the Master reminds us that anxiety has no place in our lives. How does something so impossible become possible? Through the power of faith.

Pleading with the Lord is not only accepted, it's required! Sometimes, life is hard, difficult decisions lay before us, and hardship threatens us. The Word lets us know in John 16:33 that *we will have trouble in this world, but not to worry about it because the Master, our Father, wins*! The Scripture never misleads us into thinking we will not face difficult days. In every book, we can find someone who faced days that would cause great anxiety, but in each story, we see the Lord show up!

In Daniel, we find that young man in all sorts of anxious situations. When his friends were thrown into the fiery furnace, Shadrach, Meshach, and Abednego met the Master!

They were not burned and came out smelling like roses! What was the result? King Nebuchadnezzar of Babylon, who commanded the entire nation to bow to him only a day earlier, changed his mind and demanded that their God was now his God and that all of Babylon would serve the God of Israel. God won!

Look at Jonah. We all know the story. Jonah, a prophet of God, initially refused to follow the Lord's direction and ended up being in a fish's belly and partially-digested! Despite his initial disobedience, Jonah obeyed when God sent him a second time! As he marched through Nineveh, a city known for its wickedness, shouting about the entire city being overthrown, the people fell to their knees and repented. God was already IN Nineveh when He sent Jonah. God wanted those people of Ninevah. God won!

God always wins. He always has the final say. With Babylon, Ninevah, and America, God won then, and He will win now. It might seem God has abandoned the nation, but He has not.

The second half of our Scripture says that if we refuse anxiousness, we should pray and plead with the Lord and tell Him of our worries, needs, and requests, and the outcome will be peace. How can such a thing be understood? That we can refuse anxiety? It all comes down to trust. Will you trust the pending circumstance or the Lord? Are you in a fiery furnace? Trust the Lord. Does it feel like the world is pressing? Trust the Lord.

The enemy wants you to think God cannot be trusted. He whispers lies that while God may help the other guy, He won't help you. That liar will try to convince you that you have messed up too badly, too many times, made irreparable mistakes, that God holds a grudge, and that you've done too much for God to forgive. All lies!

The truth is, God triumphed for Shadrach, Meshach, and Abednego, God triumphed for Jonah, and God will triumph for you.

WHAT TRUTH DO I NOW KNOW ABOUT GOD?

_____

_____

_____

_____

_____

_____

Is this characteristic of God an internal truth for ME?_____

- Write this characteristic on a sticky note and place it where you'll see it daily. <u>GOD NEVER FAILS</u>.

- Read the following verses on God's unfailing love and help for you: Psalm 94:18, Psalm 33:18, Psalm 143:8.

- On the following page, write down lies you've been told that have made you doubt God's unfailing love and help. Use these Scriptures to find the truth: write them down.

MY PRAYER

God, you win. I can see this to be true with Daniel, Jonah, David, and even Samson, where You used him to do business right up until the end, even though he disobeyed You. Lord, help me to know that You do not hold a grudge against me, that like with those men, You will be with me, and like their stories when You won, in my story, You will win too.

Father, help me to trust You more, to not be sucked in by the enemy's lies. When I am tempted, remind me to refuse anxiety and go to You in prayer and petitions and tell You my problems, expecting You to come to my rescue. Remind me that You win.

The liar whispers:

_____

_____

_____

_____

BUT GOD SAYS:

_____

_____

_____

_____

_____

_____

_____

_____

_____

_____

_____

_____

_____

_____

HE CAN BE TRUSTED

The LORD is my strength and my shield; in him my heart trusts, and I am helped; my heart exults, and with my song I give thanks to him.

Psalm 28:7

I have no idea how to fly an airplane. I am at a loss to explain the dials, the science behind altitude, or the ins and outs of executing a smooth landing. Nevertheless, if I need to be somewhere, I book a ticket. I arrive at the airport and check my bag, trusting it will meet me at my destination. I wait at the gate for the boarding call. Once called, I board the plane, sit down, and buckle up. I never wonder if the person in the cockpit is a pilot. I never considered how many flights they had flown or if they would get me to my destination. I never wonder if they went to pilot school or how they scored on their final exam. I simply trust the system of flying, which includes the pilot.

I would not book a ticket or board the plane if I didn't trust the pilot. I would look for an alternative method; however, getting on an airplane suggests that I, and everyone in a seat, trust the pilot and the aircraft. Furthermore, we trust that if something happens to go wrong, those in charge will know what to do and get us to safety.

The same is true for a cellphone. Unless you control the sound waves, you trust your phone. You punch words into a text and hit send, expecting the person to whom it was addressed to receive it promptly. While we cannot see the signals received by one tower, or know exactly which tower it will go to next, we trust that it will.

We don't consider the sound waves, signals, or towers; we merely trust the system. When a message fails, we don't toss the phone and say, "Well, this doesn't work. I can no longer trust cell phones."

Instead, we wait a few minutes and try again or wait until we have more bars. The bars indicate the signal, which indicates whether our message will be sent. We trust the bars, we trust the signal, we trust the system.

We are not pilots, yet we get on the plane, trusting the one who is. We are not cell towers; we send messages and make phone calls, trusting the system. We are not God, yet we pretend to be. We think we know better than He does and argue with Him about how our lives should go.

Trusting Him is a choice every time. Perhaps it is not always a conscious one, but nevertheless, we choose to trust in hundreds of situations, people, and circumstances every day. Such choices become habitual until we no longer consider whether or not they can be trusted; we simply act as though they can. God is the only One who will never fail! Busses sometimes don't run, pilots sometimes crash, phones sometimes fail, and people let us down. But God never fails. He created you and recorded all your days in a book, before you lived even one of them (Psalm 139:16). He knows you. Yet, we struggle to trust Him.

The enemy lies to us about God's trustworthiness because he knows that if we fail to trust in our Creator, our lives will be like a rudderless ship on the waves of the sea. If we are easily blown this way and that, the enemy starts huffing and puffing. He wants us to be so confused, so doubtful, so leery of God's faithfulness that he can run our lives.

The truth is, God's eye is upon you always. No matter where you go or what you do, you will not be out of the sight of God for even a moment. He had planned your days before there was even one of them, so who better to trust? Wherever you are going, He is already there.

Don't allow the enemy to persuade you that God cannot be trusted. God delights in you. He formed you; He knows you. Who better to trust?

WHAT TRUTH DO I NOW KNOW ABOUT GOD?

_____

_____

_____

_____

_____

_____

Is this characteristic of God an internal truth for ME?_____

- Write this characteristic on a sticky note and place it where you'll see it daily. GOD CAN BE TRUSTED.

- Read the following verses on God's trustworthiness: Psalm 16:11, Deuteronomy 7:9, Isaiah 26:4.

- On the following page, write down the lies you've been told that have made you question if God can be trusted. Use these Scriptures to find the truth; write them down.

MY PRAYER

Father God, sometimes I struggle to trust You. I do believe but help my unbelief. When the voices in my head tell me You won't help me, You will abandon me, or You cannot be trusted, shine a light on those things, reminding me they are lies. I don't want to believe the lies anymore. I want to know and walk in the truth, and the truth is You can be trusted in all situations of my life.

I want to trust You more and more, so secure the truth in my heart and help me be reminded daily that it is safe to trust in You.

The liar whispers:

BUT GOD SAYS:

HE KNOWS THE WAY

Trust in the LORD with all your heart, and do not lean on your own understanding. In all your ways acknowledge him, and he will make straight your paths.

Proverbs 3:5-6

In life's journey, we often encounter intersections—moments when we must choose between various paths. The uncertainty of these choices can be daunting, leaving us confused and overwhelmed, wondering which direction to take.

Praise God, we know where to go for directions. We have a promise in Proverbs 3:5-6: *Trust in the Lord with all your heart and lean not on your own understanding; in all your ways acknowledge him, and he will make your paths straight.*

The first step in following God's direction is wholeheartedly trusting His wisdom. Trusting God means placing our confidence in His character and knowing He is good, loving, and all-knowing. It requires us to abandon our desire for control and to lean into His understanding rather than our own.

Our human perspective is limited, often clouded by emotions and experiences. However, God sees the bigger picture. Isaiah 55:8-9 tells us, *For my thoughts are not your thoughts, neither are your ways my ways*, declares the Lord. This reminder encourages us to surrender our plans and seek His perfect will.

Proverbs 3:6 instructs us to *acknowledge him in all your ways*. This acknowledgment is more than a casual recognition; it is an active decision to involve God in every aspect of our lives. From major life decisions to daily routines, inviting God into our plans allows Him to shape our paths. But what does it mean to acknowledge God?

It involves seeking His guidance through prayer, meditating on His Word, and being open to His direction.

This practice fosters a deeper relationship with Him, transforming our hearts and minds to align with His will. When we acknowledge God, we cultivate a spirit of humility, recognizing that we need His wisdom to guide us.

The idea of *straight paths* suggests clarity and direction. We can confidently move forward when we follow God's guidance, knowing He is aligning our steps. Psalm 37:23 reinforces this: *The Lord makes firm the steps of the one who delights in him.* When we delight in the Lord, He aligns our desires with His purpose, guiding us along the right path.

Walking in faith means taking steps even when we cannot see the entire journey ahead. We must embrace uncertainty and trust that God's plan is unfolding. Hebrews 11:1 defines faith as *the assurance of things hoped for, the conviction of things not seen.*

As we step out in faith, we may encounter moments of doubt and fear, but we can find comfort in knowing that God is with us every step.

Consider the story of Abraham, who was called to leave his homeland without knowing his destination. He trusted God's promise and stepped out in faith, becoming the father of many nations. His journey illustrates that when we trust God, He leads us to places beyond our imagination.

However, the enemy would have us believe that we know better, that our wants and desires are the guideposts in deciding which paths to take. But this is just not so. If we choose with our hearts, we will likely end up on the wrong path and have to journey back after mistakes have been made. Some consequences are short-lived, but others are lifelong. Don't listen to the enemy. Trust God to direct you!

WHAT TRUTH DO I NOW KNOW ABOUT GOD?

_____
_____
_____
_____
_____

Is this characteristic of God an internal truth for ME?_____

- Write this characteristic on a sticky note and place it where you'll see it daily. GOD LEADS ME.

- Read the following verses on God's leading:
  Psalm 32:8, Isaiah 30:21, Hebrews 12:1.

- On the following page, write down lies you've been told that have made you wonder if God will lead you down a wrong path or if you can trust Him to lead you at all. Use these Scriptures to find the truth; write them down.

MY PRAYER

Father, I trust in You. You know the way I need to go. With all the paths before me, You know which I should take. Remind me to acknowledge and turn to You for direction at each intersection of my life; I never want to go down the wrong path. Open my ears to understanding, and give me great courage to trust You, even when the path You are leading me down seems precarious.

Help me trust You more and also trust that You will make Yourself heard by me. I've prayed so many times for You to speak to me, but You do! It is me who sometimes can't hear, or when I do hear, tend to disobey.

The liar whispers:

BUT GOD SAYS:

But overhearing what they said, Jesus said to the ruler of the synagogue, "Do not fear, only believe."

Mark 5:36

People talk. One certainly cannot point a finger across the room and say, "He's a gossip," or "She's a slanderer," because, to some degree, we are all guilty of using our tongues for ungodly uttering.

This Scripture strikes me because one can look at it from two different lenses and recognize two astounding principles.

First, let's peer through the lens of Jesus. This story comes from Mark, where a man tries to reach Jesus to plead with the Healer to touch his son. This man had just witnessed the now famous miracle of the healing of the woman who knew that if she could only touch the fringe on Jesus' garment, she would be made well. What faith!

This man had seen this, and he knew Jesus could do the same for his dying son. But before the man could reach Jesus, the man's servant popped up and told the man his son had died, so stop bothering the Master.

Well, Jesus heard the words. They were not meant for His ears, but His ears were meant for the words. As He heard them, the Healer knew the man had faith. He ignored the humanity of death and said to this man, "Don't be afraid, only believe." Jesus paid no mind to the word. For the Master, the words didn't matter. The fact that the boy had died did not cramp Jesus' style one bit. In fact, it was such a monumental moment that Mark recorded it for us to read and learn from even now.

The man's son was healed and made to live again. The circumstances seen by the human form did not matter to Christ. What the Savior was interested in was having the man believe.

Now, let's look through a second lens, a more personal one. The lens of ourselves.

How often do we look at what seems to be a final circumstance in our own lives and say, "Well, I guess it's over. We lost the war." We humans give up so easily when our senses kick in. Our soul wants to be the leader rather than our spirit. But what if we put God as the leader and followed Him?

What if, when we see a circumstance that we cannot possibly change, we say, "God's not finished yet. I will not be afraid, but I will believe." What if we begin to believe that God's plan always prevails, even when it seems impossible to us? This principle of faith and trust in God's plan can transform our perspective and give us hope in challenging situations.

How would that look? What would that change?

The enemy loves to convince us that God failed. "He doesn't care about you; He's not interested in you; He's just a big celestial being with no personal interest." Do these sound familiar to you? The list is long, but those lies lead to doubt, which leads to fear.

God says, "Do not fear, only believe!"

The truth is you are the Father's child. He looks at you, and you make Him smile. You are the child of a king and the King of the kings. He knows you and is so intensely interested and invested in you that His eyes never leave you. His thoughts of you are constant.

Do not fear; only believe.

WHAT TRUTH DO I NOW KNOW ABOUT GOD?

_____

_____

_____

_____

_____

_____

Is this characteristic of God an internal truth for ME?_____

- Write this characteristic on a sticky note and place it where you'll see it daily. GOD CARES FOR ME.

- Read the following verses about how God cares for you: Psalm 23:1-3, Isaiah 40:11, John 15:15.

- On the following page, write down the lies you've been told that have made you doubt if God cares about you. Use these Scriptures to find the truth: write them down.

MY PRAYER

Thank you for caring so much for me that there is nothing You won't do to get my attention and cause me to be like the tree planted beside the water. Lord, help me to not always listen to the whispering voices around me, often trying to lead me into doubt. Help me to be more like Jesus when He heard but ignored the naysayers and doubters. Give me eyes to see past what looks like the end and instead see what could be.

With You, Lord, there is always more, and You can be trusted. Flood me with the courage to keep believing, even when I cannot see, and stand when the enemy wants to take me down. I believe, Lord, but help my unbelief.

The liar whispers:

BUT GOD SAYS:

HE REJOICES

The LORD your God is in your midst, a mighty one who will save; he will rejoice over you with gladness; he will quiet you by his love; he will exult over you with loud singing.

Zephaniah 3:17

Who are we that God should want to be near us? Yet, He does. He chose us to belong to Him—that should be enough! Yet, it is only the beginning. He is so in love with us that He rejoices over us with joy... shouts of joy!

Where do we exhibit shouts of joy? At concerts or sporting events, usually. We have a team that, for reasons only we know, we have chosen to be "the one." We are rooting for that team. When the same team we loved only days before when they won the big game loses the next, we hang our heads, and the cheers are replaced with scorn.

This is not the Lord's response when we choose sin, disappointing everyone and even letting ourselves down. Even then, the Lord rejoices over us with shouts of joy. He is our victorious warrior, and He knows what we do not—that we will get up, press on, and grow in faith and hope in Him.

He loves us not because of what we do for Him, for indeed, there is nothing we can do to earn such a love that the Father lavishes on us. He loves us because of who He is. We could work our fingers to the bone, give all we have to the poor, and sacrifice everything to go to a foreign land to share His name, but none of this would cause the Father to love us more than He already does. He loves us completely, a full measure.

He chose us because His love for us was so great, so overflowing, so full that He could not NOT choose us. He sacrificed His own Son so that He could adopt you. He wanted us as His children. He wanted to dwell with us, walk with us, and pour all He has onto us.

We do not even understand love, really. All we know is a human version that is incredibly flawed and badly broken. It is like taking the most beautiful, extravagant crystal vase ever to be seen and smashing it on the floor, then picking up a tiny fragment of that vase, which has no more shine and no more value, holding it up and saying, "See? This is the vase." It is not!

Yet, that is what we do with love. We think we understand love because we have a shard of a very broken vase. But He is the vase. He is love. We cannot begin to understand His love for us because we know love only in broken pieces and fragments.

So, when the enemy lies and whispers that we are unloveable, that God cannot possibly love us, or that God is far from us, we must say, "My God actually rejoices over me with great shouts of joy! My Father chose me, and He is always in my midst."

God is love, and there is no brokenness in Him. He is right here, among us, and we have an open door to be as close to Him as we desire. The closer we get to the Father, the more we can understand an unbroken, undeserved, unearned love. That is how He loves us. We love Him because He first loved us.

The truth is that while we were still walking in sin, living in darkness, still His enemy, He reached in and chose us and said, "This one's mine." And regardless of how broken we may feel while on this earth, the Father never changes His mind about us.

Trust Him to keep you, guard you, tell you the truth, and never let you go or give up on you. God will never un-choose you. His love is constant, unwavering, and unconditional. He chose you, and He will never change His mind about you.

WHAT TRUTH DO I NOW KNOW ABOUT GOD?

_____

_____

_____

_____

_____

_____

Is this characteristic of God an internal truth for ME?_____

- Write this characteristic on a sticky note and place it where you'll see it daily. GOD REJOICES OVER ME.

- Read the following verses on God rejoicing over you: Psalm 147:11, John 15:9, Psalm 35:27.

- On the following page, write down the lies you've been told that have made you doubt if God rejoices over you. Use these Scriptures to find the truth: write them down.

MY PRAYER

Father, You chose me. It's hard for me to believe such a thing because when I look at how often I fail and how sinful I am, I wonder how You could! How could a loving and perfect King love one like me? Yet, Your Word says You do, and so You must. I know the Word is truth, so help me to simply believe that Your love for me is because of who You are, not because of who I am.

That concept seems so foreign, Lord, but I know You will help my mind believe it and my heart receive it. Thank you for loving me with perfect love. Help me to give up trying to understand it and simply accept it.

The liar whispers:

_____

_____

_____

_____

_____

BUT GOD SAYS:

_____

_____

_____

_____

_____

_____

_____

_____

_____

_____

_____

_____

_____

_____

_____

HE DESIGNS

For we are his workmanship, created in Christ Jesus for good works, which God prepared beforehand, that we should walk in them.

Ephesians 2:10

Our lives are not mere happenstance. We are more than the sum of our days or a collection of moments. We were made for a purpose by a God who knows us intimately, even if we don't know Him at all.

The Bible says this God—this King of the kings—counts the number of hairs on our heads (Luke 12:7). He knows our thoughts, even before we form them (Psalm 139:2). He's known us before we were a cell in our mother's womb (Jeremiah 1:5). It is this God who has created us in His image. He formed the story of our lives, which He wrote before the book even opened to the first page, and He made plans for our lives to matter, to make a difference in this world of indifference.

His knowledge of us is not just a mere acquaintance but an intimate understanding of our deepest thoughts and desires.

How do we know this to be true when the enemy whispers lies, trying to convince us we don't matter and have no purpose in this world? How do we combat the whispers that say our lives are insignificant, that what happens between our first breath and our last makes no difference and leaves no impact?

I am sure you've heard those words harassing your mind at one time or another, as have I. But they are lies of the fallen one, who wants only to ruin our lives, break us, and drag us away to where he is going. But he is a liar.

The truth is that God Himself took great care to create us as He wanted us to be.

The world has broken us down, but God puts forth His hand and says, "Get up, Child. I have things for you to do, great and marvelous plans for your days. I have a plan and a purpose for your life." He is the great Craftsman, and we are His workmanship. His plans for us are not ordinary but extraordinary, filled with hope and inspiration.

One rarely ponders such a word as *workmanship*; it is skimmed over without letting the depth of its meaning sink into our souls. But stop and think about the word used to describe us. We are not just a creation but a masterpiece, meticulously crafted by the hands of the Almighty.

A skilled craftsman creates a beautiful product in whatever area of their craft in which they are skilled. A cabinet craftsman painstakingly builds strong, elegant, beautiful cabinets that make whoever looks at them want to run their hands over the smooth finishes and take in the smell of the wood. The cabinet craftsman might take hours to carve intricate details into the wood. He may use his scroll saw to round edges or an artist's brush to ensure stain settles in even the tiniest crevice.

We are His workmanship; He created us with a purpose in mind. The God who created the Heavens, who set the stars in place with precision, knows where the snow is kept, and commands the lightning, is the Master Creator, and His workmanship is found in you! If He set the stars in place, as we see in Psalm 8:3, and calls them out night after night by name (Isaiah 40:26), how much more does He put His craftsmanship into you? The stars are for light, but you are for Him.

Do not be deceived. God created you with a purpose and things to do. He will lead you to those things and ensure your purpose is fulfilled. We only need to walk with Him, stay near Him, and fill our minds with His truth. The rest is up to Him.

WHAT TRUTH DO I NOW KNOW ABOUT GOD?

_____

_____

_____

_____

_____

Is this characteristic of God an internal truth for ME?_____

- Write this characteristic on a sticky note and place it where you'll see it daily. <u>GOD DESIGNED ME</u>.

- Read the following verses on God's design for you: Psalm 139:14, Isaiah 64:8, Genesis 2:7.

- On the following page, write down the lies you've been told that have made you think you were an accident, or not important or valuable. Use these Scriptures to find the truth: write them down.

MY PRAYER

How absolutely amazing You are, Lord. Of the billions of people on this earth, and all that has gone before and all who will come after, You carefully designed each one, and You know each one entirely. How beyond my understanding You are. You are the Chief Craftsman, and I am Your workmanship.

You know every detail of my life, yet You love me. Before I knew You, You loved me. Help my mind to understand the depths of Your love for me so that I can walk from that place of being loved by the King.

The liar whispers:

BUT GOD SAYS:

HE CALLS

But you are a chosen race, a royal priesthood, a holy nation, a people for his own possession, that you may proclaim the excellencies of him who called you out of darkness into his marvelous light.

1 Peter 2:9

You have been chosen. The One who created everything simply by commanding it is so stood before time and looked at the expanse of all time from the beginning until the end, and He saw you. In that moment, He chose you to belong to Him past the end of time for eternity. Ten million years from now, immeasurable and inconceivable, you will still belong to Him because before you existed, He chose you.

When the words of this verse were first spoken, they were given to Israel. God wanted Israel to belong to Him, but they were stubborn people who rejected Him. But because God is love, His love was not limited to the Israelites. He wouldn't let their rejection stop Him from having those He loved as His own. And so, He expanded the borders to include the Gentiles—to include you and me.

Now, we are grafted into His kingdom (Romans 11:24), so all that was reserved for the Israelites is now made available to those who believe in Christ and receive Him as their Savior.

If that's you, then He chose you! John 15:16 tells us that we did not choose Him, but He chose us. He loved us first, and now we get to love Him back. He always makes the first move, and we respond with the grace He provides us. Everything starts with the King.

Think of a time, perhaps as a child, when you were in the dark. It can be scary in the dark, especially when we are unsure what else is in the dark. Maybe in your home it's not terrifying if the power goes out and it is suddenly black, and you must feel your way to the drawer where you stashed the flashlight. You know what's in the dark and can haphazardly move toward the light.

But what about if you are in unfamiliar surroundings? Think of being in the woods, and you are a bit lost. You've never been there before, and you don't know what's behind the next bend in the trail. Suddenly, the sun goes down, and you are there, in the blackness, unable to find your way out. You might be able to feel a tree, but you'll stumble over the rock in the way, fall, and skin your knees because you couldn't see the rock. There are eery sounds you don't recognize; the dark is dangerous then. And this is merely physical darkness.

The darkness that the Lord is referring to is even darker! He is speaking about spiritual darkness, the darkness of walking through this world without His light to illuminate the path before us. He knows the way, and He is the light. Because He chose you, you will never walk in spiritual darkness. The Scripture says, *Thy Word is a lamp to my feet and a light to my path* (Psalm 119:105).

He has chosen you to bring you from that dark place from which you could never have found your way and transplanted you in the eternal light, illuminating your path, directing your feet, showing you which way to go. Now, the King, the everlasting light, will surround you for all of your days until you pass from this limited world where time constrains, to the one where the light will radiate and time will be no more. There, darkness will be eliminated because where He is, darkness is not.

The enemy will try and tell you this is not so, and he will bring countless temptations to persuade you that the darkness is good. The darkness is where the fun is, where wealth can be found, and where popularity is easy. But these are lies; these are traps to lead you from the light back into the dark places. Don't listen.

Keep your eyes on the light, on the King, and He will lead you. He will lead you into good places where the darkness cannot go. He will give you hope and a future. He will fill you with peace, and when this life is over, He will say as you look upon His face, "Welcome Home, child."

WHAT TRUTH DO I NOW KNOW ABOUT GOD?

_____

_____

_____

_____

_____

_____

Is this characteristic of God an internal truth for ME?_____

- Write this characteristic on a sticky note and place it where you'll see it daily. GOD CALLS ME.

- Read the following verses on God's calling of you: Hebrews 3:1, Ephesians 1:3-5, Jeremiah 1:5-8.

- On the following page, write down the lies you've been told that God can't use you, that you are too broken for Him to do anything profitable with. Use these Scriptures to find the truth; write them down.

MY PRAYER

Thank You for choosing me. It was not because I deserved to be chosen but because You are good. Thank You that You have called me out of the darkness and into Your light, which will never dim or fade. Open my understanding to know more about how valuable that light is. Thank you that You have chosen me for a purpose and that it's not up to me to make anything happen; it's my job to trust and obey.

Don't let me miss out on anything You've planned for me. Open my eyes to see opportunities that I might otherwise miss. According to Your Word, thank you for making all things work together for my good because I love You.

The liar whispers:

_____
_____
_____
_____
_____

BUT GOD SAYS:

_____
_____
_____
_____
_____
_____
_____
_____
_____
_____
_____
_____
_____
_____
_____

HE GIVES A FUTURE

Brothers, I do not consider that I have made it my own. But one thing I do: forgetting what lies behind and straining forward to what lies ahead, I press on toward the goal for the prize of the upward call of God in Christ Jesus.

Philippians 3:13-14

Uncertainty is sometimes a part of life, and the idea of a hopeful future can occasionally seem elusive. Yet, we have assurance that God gives us a future filled with purpose and promise. Philippians 3:13-14 serves as a reminder to let go of the things in our past that hold us there. One cannot hold tightly to the past while trying to move ahead to the future.

The journey toward a hopeful future begins with letting go of the things from the past. Paul emphasizes the importance of forgetting what lies behind. This doesn't mean erasing our memories or ignoring our experiences; instead, it suggests releasing the burden of past failures, regrets, and accomplishments that might keep us from moving forward.

Often, we carry burdens from our past—mistakes we've made, failed relationships, or broken dreams. These can create a sense of paralysis, making it tough to imagine a brighter future. However, God calls us to release these burdens and trust Him with our past. In Isaiah 43:18-19, God declares, *Forget the former things; do not dwell on the past. See, I am doing a new thing!* This promise reassures us that God is always working, designing new beginnings from our brokenness.

While letting go of the past is essential, we must also engage with the present. Paul writes, *I press on toward the goal*. This indicates an active pursuit of our calling through intentionality and determination. God gives us a future, but we must take steps toward it daily, trusting Him as we go.

Each day is an opportunity to align our lives with His purpose.

James 1:5 directs us to *ask for wisdom and believe God will supply* it because the Scripture says He will give generously to all who ask if they believe. By seeking God's wisdom, we can steer our circumstances with clarity and purpose, allowing Him to guide us toward our future.

God's promise of a future is not merely about what lies ahead but also about the transformation He works in us on the journey. As we press on, we become more like Christ, growing in character and faith. God reminds us that all things work together for the good of those who love Him. (Romans 8:28) This promise reminds us that our future is intricately linked to God's purpose for our lives, making it a future we want to seek after.

The future God gives us is not about personal aspirations only but also about participating in His kingdom work. Ephesians 2:10 tells us that we were *created to do good works* and that *God prepared these things for us in advance*. Each of us has a role in God's grand narrative.

Straining toward what is ahead suggests that moving ahead requires effort, perseverance, and a commitment to follow God's lead. There will be challenges, but we are not alone. The Holy Spirit empowers us, guiding us through every trial and triumph.

The enemy would have us believe lies, though, that we have somehow canceled out our future by bad choices, broken pasts, or simply because God doesn't care. But we know these are lies and must not let them take root in our minds.

The truth is that God has planned your future. We all fail and have things in our past that are hard to forget, but with the grace of God, we can lay down that broken past and, with both hands, grab on to the future that the Lord has laid before us, trusting Him to lead us one step at a time.

WHAT TRUTH DO I NOW KNOW ABOUT GOD?

_____

_____

_____

_____

_____

Is this characteristic of God an internal truth for ME?_____

- Write this characteristic on a sticky note and place it where you'll see it daily. GOD HAS A FUTURE FOR ME.

- Read the following verses on God planning your future: Jeremiah 29:11, Philippians 1:6, Proverbs 19:21.

- On the following page, write down the lies you've been told that have made you doubt that God has a future and a purpose for you.. Use these Scriptures to find the truth: write them down.

MY PRAYER

Father, I desire to move ahead with You. My life has been bound by the past, by hurts and rejection from others. Give me the courage to set those things down and stop dragging them into my present. Help me to forgive those who hurt me, even if they don't acknowledge it, and ask for forgiveness from those to whom I've caused pain.

Give me the tenacity to strive forward, to let go of my past so I can have empty hands to grab hold of my future. You have great plans for me, Father, and I want to walk in all the ways of You. Teach me to do that and remind me when I am tempted to pick up old hurts that what is ahead is far greater than what I'm leaving behind.

The liar whispers: _____

_____

_____

_____

_____

BUT GOD SAYS: _____

_____

_____

_____

_____

_____

_____

_____

_____

_____

_____

_____

_____

_____

_____

_____

HE PROVIDES

And my God will supply every need of yours according to his riches in glory in Christ Jesus.

Philippians 4:19

What is your need today? We have so many that narrowing it down to one can be tricky. Sometimes, a need is tangible, but often, it is something we cannot hold in our hands, such as peace or wisdom. Other times, there is a need so pressing that it is causing sleepless nights and great anxiety within us.

This is never good news, but then again, it is. The Lord always knows better than we what our needs are. We say, "Lord, I need ... such and such," but the Lord quietly whispers back, "Child, I know what you need more than you do. Trust Me."

What did Abraham possibly need when taking his promised son to the mountain to sacrifice? He needed faith and a lamb, and God provided both. What did Paul and Silas need when in prison? They needed to trust in the Master and for the doors to burst open, and God provided both.

How about the mother of Moses when the decree went out that would take the life of her sweet boy? She needed to believe in her King; she needed her baby hidden, and God provided both. We all have many significant needs, and God provides for each of them in His timing and ways.

Paul and Silas could have begged the Lord to free them, to declare that they were innocent, merely servants of God. Why would a God whom they served so wholeheartedly allow them to suffer? Instead, they sang songs in the midnight hour, and out of nowhere, God opened the doors. Paul and Silas obeyed God, trusting He would provide the answer and their desired freedom, and He did.

What about the Mamma of Moses? She must have been shattered to watch her son be found by the Egyptians—their mortal enemy—by the ones who were tormenting her people. Indeed, she begged God to help. He did! He organized it so she could be the nursemaid for her son, getting to snuggle and pray over and teach him in her own household. God had a bigger purpose for Moses, which was to lead all the Israelites out of captivity; thus, Moses needed to be in the inner circle of the Egyptians. Mamma obeyed God, trusting He would provide an answer for her son, and He did.

God does not always provide the answer we want because we see it in small pieces. We see only what is right in front of us. We see our own comfort, and that is all we can understand. God sees the whole picture; our comfort is not His top priority. His purpose is not singular. It is not to fix every problem we ever encounter. That would make Him a magic genie, which He is not. He is God Almighty!

Notice this verse says the parameters in which God will supply your need in the "according to" part. No clause is included that says He will meet your need, "According to your performance," "According to your righteousness," or "According to your deservedness." This is where the enemy whispers his lies.

"You need to jump through 149 hoops before God will help you. You must fast more, pray longer, and earn God's help. You do not deserve God's help." And on and on the liar's list goes. We become frustrated when we entertain the liar, thinking that perhaps the whispers are true. After all, we told that little lie last week, so indeed, we don't deserve the help of the King of kings. If God was going to meet our needs according to anything on our end, no need would ever be met.

The truth is that God meets our needs based on HIS riches in Heaven, to which there is no limit. God is limitless in His need-meeting capabilities BECAUSE it has nothing to do with us and everything to do with Him.

WHAT TRUTH DO I NOW KNOW ABOUT GOD?

_____

_____

_____

_____

_____

_____

Is this characteristic of God an internal truth for ME?_____

- Write this characteristic on a sticky note and place it where you'll see it daily. <u>GOD PROVIDES FOR ME</u>.

- Read the following verses on God's provision for you: Matthew 6:31, 33, James 1:17, Psalm 34:8-10.

- On the following page, write down the lies you've been told that have made you doubt that God will provide for you. Use these Scriptures to find the truth: write them down.

MY PRAYER

Provider, You know of every area in my life where I need help, and You know more than I do what I need. Draw me closer to Your heart so I can trust You more. Remind me of the times in my past when You met a need I could not meet myself.

Bring stories to mind from the Word where You met a need of someone that I can relate to. Thank you that You meet my needs according to Your riches, not my deservedness. Thank you for choosing me to know You and for allowing me to have needs so that I can learn more to trust You, my Provider.

The liar whispers:

_____

_____

_____

_____

_____

BUT GOD SAYS:

_____

_____

_____

_____

_____

_____

_____

_____

_____

_____

_____

_____

_____

_____

_____

HE QUALIFIES

... giving thanks to the Father, who has qualified you to share in the inheritance of the saints in light. He has delivered us from the domain of darkness and transferred us to the kingdom of his beloved Son, in whom we have redemption, the forgiveness of sins.

Colossians 1:12-14

Have you ever received an inheritance? It's a bittersweet conundrum because while receiving such a gift is wonderful, it usually means the recipient lost someone they dearly loved. Someone had to lose their life for an inheritance to be gained; that's just how it works, and there's no way around it. Most often, the recipient is a family member. This means that to share in that inheritance, they must have been a part of the family.

This Scripture assures us that we receive an inheritance of the most extraordinary measure: eternal life in Heaven with God. How can this be so? Because there was a death! The death of Jesus on the cross meant there was an inheritance. It is not available to just anyone, though. Only we who believe Jesus is the Son of God qualify for such a sacrificial gift. We must be members of His family to be qualified.

In earthly circumstances, the recipient receives the gift without having earned it. How? By acknowledging they are who they claim to be and demonstrating they are the ones to whom the deceased has left the gift. The recipient did nothing to earn it, nothing to deserve it, other than being named on the will.

Likewise, with the Father, He qualified us to share in the inheritance. How? The rest of the verse answers that. He rescues us from the realm of darkness where the enemy lies in wait to snare and drag us all away and transfers us into the Kingdom of His Son.

What is required of us? To believe! According to John 1:12, once we believe in His name, God gives us the right to become His child and share in His eternal inheritance. This belief is our assurance, confidence, and ticket to the most significant inheritance.

Think deeply about this. Pause, take a minute, and picture it. We were caught in darkness. Ensnared in a trap of our making. We were born into slavery because we were born into a sinful world. We needed a way out, but how does one without power over such things find redemption without a redeemer? How can we ever receive an inheritance of eternal freedom, redemption, and life unless there is a death?

Oh, but there is a way. The One who had no sin, the only One not born into sin, that sinless, perfect Christ gave His life to become sin, accepting the death required so that we could receive such an inheritance.

Once there was death, a way could be made for anyone who believed that the One who died was who He said He was, the Son of the eternal, uncreated God, to be transferred. Death allowed the inheritance, and the resurrection offered the transfer.

The enemy's whispers want to lead us back into captivity by trying to convince us that we must earn such a gift. If not silenced with truth, those lies cause us to find imaginary hoops to jump, such as performing certain rituals, achieving a certain level of righteousness, or proving our worthiness, so we wear ourselves out and miss out on the joy of such an inheritance.

But the truth is, Christ died to make the inheritance available; God offers us a way to become part of His family so we can become heirs of that inheritance. He does the work; we receive the blessing. All one must do is believe.

WHAT TRUTH DO I NOW KNOW ABOUT GOD?

_____

_____

_____

_____

_____

_____

Is this characteristic of God an internal truth for ME?_____

- Write this characteristic on a sticky note and place it where you'll see it daily. GOD QUALIFIES ME.

- Read the following verses on God qualifying you:
  2 Corinthians 3:5, Ephesians 2:10, 1 Corinthians 1:27-28.

- On the following page, write down the lies you've been told that have made you doubt you are useful to God. Use these Scriptures to find the truth: write them down.

MY PRAYER

You have qualified me for an inheritance and to be a part of Your family and kingdom. Praise You, Lord! Who could fathom such a thing? You looked at me and said, "Yes, that one is mine, and nothing can stop what I will do in that life." Lord, I don't deserve anything, yet You offer me everything. As a King's child, You give me access to all You have! Lord, I can't wrap my mind around such a thing, and all I can do is say thank you!

Grow me into the person You desire me to be, and teach me to love You more, to seek You often, and to know You deeper. Father, You are good to me, and I am grateful.

REFLECTIONS

The liar whispers:

_____

_____

_____

_____

BUT GOD SAYS:

_____

_____

_____

_____

_____

_____

_____

_____

_____

_____

_____

_____

_____

_____

HE INVITES

Let us then with confidence draw near to the throne of grace, that we may receive mercy and find grace to help in time of need.

Hebrews 4:16

If you could choose anyone on earth from whom you'd like to receive a dinner invitation, who would it be? What would you do with the invitation: read it and toss it away, frame it, or laminate it? How excited would we be to know what that person thought of us? How would you prepare for that dinner? What would you wear? Who would you share the news with?

The Mighty God Himself has extended an open invitation to His throne of grace! We can come anytime, for anything, and just stay there. We never have to leave. We don't have to beg for an invite or prepare ourselves to be in His presence. He says, "Come on in."

At the heart of this invitation is the notion of God's throne of grace. Unlike an earthly throne, which might symbolize power and authority, God's throne represents His boundless love, mercy, and grace. It is where we can come just as we are, without pretense or hesitation.

Approaching God's throne with confidence means shedding our insecurities and recognizing that we are accepted by Him. This confidence is not based on our righteousness but Christ's finished work. *In him and through faith in him we may approach God with freedom and confidence.* (Ephesians 3:12)

We often feel unworthy when thinking about approaching God. We may be reminded of our past mistakes or overwhelmed by our current struggles. However, God invites us to come confidently, reminding us that His grace is sufficient for our shortcomings. We can go just as we are; no strings are attached.

Jesus tells the weary, *Come to me, all you who are weary and burdened, and I will give you rest* (Matthew 11:28). This is an open invitation to lay down our burdens and find comfort in Him. It's an assurance that God does not turn us away; He welcomes us with wide-open arms.

The invitation to approach God's throne comes with a promise: we will receive mercy and find grace. Mercy is God's compassion for us in our failures, while grace is His unmerited favor. Together, they form the foundation of our relationship with Him.

When we have emotional, spiritual, or physical needs, we can come to God, knowing He understands our struggles. God is intimately aware of our needs and invites us to bring them before Him.

God's invitation is not only for moments of crisis; it extends to every aspect of our lives. He desires a relationship that thrives on communication and intimacy. Cultivating this requires intentionality. Spending time in prayer, reading Scripture, and meditating on His Word allows us to draw closer to Him. Each moment spent in His presence deepens our understanding of His character and fills us with His peace.

The liar would try to tell us that we aren't good enough to enter God's presence, that we have to clean up our act first, or that we are too dirty. The enemy detests that God has given us an open invitation, so he works hard to make us believe the invitation isn't for us.

Oh, but it is! The invitation to approach the throne of God is for all of His children. Every Believer is invited, and no reservation is required. The choice is ours, whether to join Him in His throneroom or sit out in the hallway recounting our own sin that He doesn't even see. Don't waste one more minute looking backward at your past when the Father is in front of you, waiting.

WHAT TRUTH DO I NOW KNOW ABOUT GOD?

Is this characteristic of God an internal truth for ME?_____

- Write this characteristic on a sticky note and place it where you'll see it daily. GOD INVITED ME.

- Read the following verses on God inviting you: Matthew 11:28, Mark 6:31, John 3:16.

- On the following page, write down the lies you've been told that have made you think God's invitation does not apply to you, or that you are too unworthy. Use these Scriptures to find the truth; write them down.

MY PRAYER

It's greater than my mind can conceive that You, the King of Heaven, have invited me not only into Your kingdom but into Your family. Lord, You don't wait until I am righteous on my own to invite me. I don't have to work or give my way in; You invite me because I belong to You.

Lord, thank you for seeking me, for giving me ears to hear, eyes to see, and a heart that needs You. Thank you for calling me and loving me first. Please give me the courage to believe I have been invited because of Your grace and not my works. Help me to always be aware of Your grace toward me and not take it for granted.

The liar whispers:

_____

_____

_____

_____

BUT GOD SAYS:

_____

_____

_____

_____

_____

_____

_____

_____

_____

_____

_____

_____

_____

HE MAKES A WAY

It is the LORD who goes before you. He will be with you; he will not leave you or forsake you. Do not fear or be dismayed."

Deuteronomy 31:8

Scripture reveals God as our refuge and strength, our strong tower in which we can hide, our salvation, shield, and more—each title reflects His unwavering protection over His people. Jesus, the Good Shepherd, shows His profound love by laying down His life for His sheep, guarding them against the dangers that would come to attack.

In Christ, we find protection and peace, resting in the assurance that we are shielded from harm. Though suffering and persecution may arise, the promise of God's salvation remains steadfast and sure. He can be trusted, even in the hard times.

What is required of us to be under His protection? In Exodus 14:13-14, Moses finds himself leading—or trying to lead—the Israelites across the sea. However, the sea is enormous, with no boats or bridges. Furthermore, the Egyptian army is behind them, about to overtake them. What does Moses say? What is the advice of the leader whom God chose for such a task?

"Just hold on guys. Stand there and wait. God will fight for you. These guys who you can see coming at you now, with the swords and daggers, don't worry about it. You're never going to see them again. Just stand there and wait."

Can you imagine such a thing? Wait for what? To lose our heads? To watch our children be dragged away? What are we waiting for, exactly, oh mighty leader?" Can you hear them? I can hear the women wailing, the men cursing, and the children shrieking. The way ahead leads to death by drowning; the way back welcomes death by sword. Wait for what, Moses?

But God had been with Moses. He had delivered life-giving water from a rock, food from the air, a cloud by day, and a fire by night. Moses may not have known the exact method God would use to solve this particular problem. Still, he'd watched that same God deliver them from less terrifying but equally important life-threatening circumstances before, so Moses trusted that God would do it again.

His faith in God's protection was unwavering, and he believed.

There are numerous times in Scripture where we are instructed about the strong shield of the Lord. Each time, it tells us to whom that shield is readily available: those who take refuge in Him. Now, nobody would take shelter in a precarious and shaky rock when looking for where to hide as a storm approached. We would not stand beneath a branch about to fall or a cliff ready to give way. How silly.

In a storm, one would look for a stable place to take refuge—a shelter that would hold fast and not fail. God is that refuge in such storms of life.

It seems that storms come often, but the Bible never suggests they won't. The life of a Believer is not one protected from the storms but one protected in the storms. One can never know how the Lord might act when one of His children is facing a storm, but we know He will act. All we need to do is stay close to the Master to take refuge in Him.

We are not responsible for calming the storm or running around looking for a hiding place. Our responsibility is to go to the One who has promised to be our shelter and rest in the knowledge that He will be.

WHAT TRUTH DO I NOW KNOW ABOUT GOD?

Is this characteristic of God an internal truth for ME?_____

- Write this characteristic on a sticky note and place it where you'll see it daily. GOD MAKES A WAY FOR ME.

- Read the following verses on God's way making: Isaiah 43:19, Isaiah 41:13, John 14:6.

- On the following page, write down the lies you've been told that have made you think you were on your own, and God has abandoned you. Use these Scriptures to find the truth: write them down.

MY PRAYER

Wherever I am, You are with me. Thank you that You are there in all situations. When I face my days, whether good or bad, You are with me. Thank you. Like the Israelites at sea, sometimes it seems I am standing in an impossible situation; I can't move ahead and I can't go back. In those days and all the days between, please remind me You are with me. You have already gone ahead and worked it all out.

Give me the courage to move ahead, knowing You have the situation in Your control, even if I cannot see the way through.

The liar whispers:

_____

_____

_____

_____

_____

BUT GOD SAYS:

_____

_____

_____

_____

_____

_____

_____

_____

_____

_____

_____

_____

_____

_____

HE FORGIVES

If we confess our sins, he is faithful and just to forgive us our sins and to cleanse us from all unrighteousness.

1 John 1:9

Guilt and shame are heavy. Nobody can carry them for long without negatively impacting our lives. They are accusatory, reminding us of our failures with a "How could you ..." attached. Guilt and shame are not from God; they are tools of the enemy skillfully used to keep us chained to our past, crippling us from moving ahead with the Lord and His plans for our lives. We cannot carry them. They weren't meant for us.

The Father did not allow the death of His Son so that we could carry what He died to forgive. The Great I AM is the embodiment of forgiveness to all who ask of Him. We can come in humble repentance, acknowledging our sin and our need for Christ to forgive us and give Him the guilt and shame we have attached to the behavior.

The Word is clear that we all have sinned and fall short of God's glory (Romans 3:23). But it is equally as clear in the very next verse that although we were sinners, when we come to Him and ask to be forgiven, we are! In the exact moment we go to Him, He washes us clean. We immediately become justified by His gift of grace.

In that exact moment, the enemy snatches that sin for which we've been forgiven and throws it back at us to see if it will stick. But we are covered in the oil of the Holy Spirit, so the only way that guilt or shame will stick and hang on is if we pick it back up.

Sometimes, we have difficulty forgiving ourselves, but when we realize the depth of God's love and the extent to which He went to offer us complete forgiveness, we find it necessary to trust in His forgiveness and, by grace, receive it. The forgiveness of the Father cannot be earned, only received.

Being forgiven gives us great freedom; it removes the barrier between God and us. When we hurt another person, even if that person forgives us, we walk a little more sheepishly for a time because we may feel badly knowing we hurt someone. However, we know that as humans, we don't forget past hurts. We cannot somehow remove them from our memories and move ahead like they never happened.

But God can, and He does. In Psalm 103:12, the Lord removes our sin as far as the East is from the West. In Hebrews 8:12, God tells us that *He will be merciful and remember our sins no more*. There are plenty of verses that give similar promises. God, in His everlasting grace, chooses not to remember our sins. What grace the Father gives to His children.

If He no longer remembers them, we ought not to, either. While this might take some work on our part, we can ask Him to help us forget our past and not drag it with us into the present.

While the enemy will persist for a time with his lying and hurling guilt and shame at us, we can choose to let it bounce off and fall into the sea, where the Lord throws our sin. We can believe the truth that Jesus' death on the cross was sufficient, that our debt of sin has been paid in full, and that God sees us as righteous, welcoming us into His presence without shame or guilt. We can stand, without judgment, before our King.

WHAT TRUTH DO I NOW KNOW ABOUT GOD?

_____

_____

_____

_____

_____

_____

Is this characteristic of God an internal truth for ME?_____

- Write this characteristic on a sticky note and place it where you'll see it daily. <u>GOD FORGAVE ME</u>.

- Read the following verses on God's forgiveness for you: Hebrews 8:12, Ephesians 1:7, Colossians 1:13-14.

- On the following page, write down the lies you've been told that have made you doubt God's forgiveness and causes you to carry guilt and shame. Use these Scriptures to find the truth: write them down.

MY PRAYER

Jesus, I don't want to carry guilt anymore. It's a heavy burden You never intended for me to drag through life. Shut my ears to the lies of the enemy that try to convince me to be ashamed. You forgave me, so I am no longer guilty of my past. Remind me of the truth: that I am a forgiven child of the King of Heaven, and You don't hold me accountable for my past.

Lord, lead me to You, and never give up on me. You have forgiven me and paid my debt, and I am free! Help me to disengage from my past behavior. You love me exactly as I am right now. You called me for a purpose, and I can't walk in my identity as a child of the King when all I can think of is the shame of my past. I give it all to You now.

The liar whispers:

BUT GOD SAYS:

HE NEVER LEAVES

Keep your life free from the love of money, and be content with what you have, for he has said, "I will never leave you nor forsake you."

Hebrews 13:5

You are not alone. Not for a single moment of any day are you without the presence of the King with you. This truth may not always be easy to grasp in a world that often leaves us feeling isolated or abandoned. It's confusing how we struggle with loneliness in a world of over 8 billion people. The worst kind of loneliness, in fact, grips us when we are in the middle of a crowd.

We often confuse being alone with being lonely. However, once we realize the truth of God's constant presence with us, we can better combat the loneliness we all experience from time to time.

The enemy preys on our weaknesses, and loneliness is a common human vulnerability. He whispers, "See? Everyone has left. You are alone." Loneliness comes not from being physically alone but from the lie that you have nobody. These lies tempt our hearts when we look around and see no one. But remember, the truth is found in the Word of God. It's where we can always turn to combat the enemy's lies and extinguish his fiery darts.

In our current world, a genuine mental health crisis blankets those of us who feel like we have been abandoned in this world, as though we are walking blindly through life trying to make it work, with no one to walk beside us.

When we feel we have no one to give us direction, hug us when we are sad, pick us up when we stumble, rejoice with us in our successes, or wipe our tears when they fall, life becomes burdensome and lonely. From scars on one's soul when they were left behind by a parent, abandoned by a spouse, or forgotten as a child comes a fear of abandonment and being alone.

The enemy preys on weakness, so when an event occurs that triggers that wound, the enemy manipulates and pokes to try and convince us that lies are true and that the earlier event that invaded our soul in the past, determines who we are in the present.

We may hear things such as, "Nobody wants you" or "Leave them before they leave you." He uses lies to try and convince us that we are unlovable and that everyone leaves. He deceives us into putting up walls, ensuring no one ever gets in or gets close to us. We close our hearts, determined never to be hurt again. He pummels our minds with thoughts of "You're not good enough, nobody likes you," and the lies go round and round.

But those whispers are lies. Repeated enough times, we become deceived into believing those lies are true, and we begin to repeat them to ourselves, further cementing them into our minds and hearts. We begin to form our worldview around those lies, resulting in living from them: making life choices from fear of those lies rather than peace in the truth of God's Word.

We can be confident that God's Word is always true; we can trust it to be the foundation upon which our personal perspective of ourselves can be built. So, when the Word of God says that the Lord Himself will never desert us, leave us, or abandon us, we can believe it. We can build our worldview on that fact. We can make choices based on the trustworthy Word of God. Once the truth of it becomes living and active in our mind and soul, we find healing and can easily shut down the whisperings of the enemy's lies.

Don't mistake this as meaning there will not be difficult times, but in those times of deep water, where you will not be drowned and fiery furnaces in which you will not be burned, you will not face them alone. The Lord will stand with you. He will be your defender. He will be your guide. He will be your protector. He will stay with you and strengthen you to overcome. He will never leave, never abandon, never withdraw.

WHAT TRUTH DO I NOW KNOW ABOUT GOD?

_____

_____

_____

_____

_____

_____

Is this characteristic of God an internal truth for ME?_____

- Write this characteristic on a sticky note and place it where you'll see it daily. <u>GOD WILL NOT ABANDON ME</u>.

- Read the following verses on God's constant presence: Psalm 139:7, 1 Corinthians 3:16, John 15:5.

- On the following page, write down the lies you've been told that have made you believe the Lord will abandon you. Use these Scriptures to find the truth; write them down.

MY PRAYER

Father, sometimes I struggle with feeling alone. It sometimes feels like nobody is with me and that I am just wandering through this life by myself. Open the eyes of my soul to see You standing with me. Remind me that You will never leave me to walk by myself.

Lord, bring people to surround me, like-minded friends. While I know You are with me, it would be great to have others in physical form with whom I could share things. Bring those who will always point to You and remind me that You are in my midst.

The liar whispers:

BUT GOD SAYS:

HE IS PEACE

You keep him in perfect peace whose mind is stayed on you, because he trusts in you.

Isaiah 26:3

The country is currently in torrents of unrest. It was also a mess in Jesus' day and most of the days in between. Which country, you might ask, to which the answer would be all of them. Our world is in a state that seems out of control. But it's not. In this chaotic world, God is in control. He is still sitting on the throne, and while all seems lost, it isn't.

Where can peace be found? Not in any earthly thing. Inflation, war, rumors of war, unstable weather, broken governments, broken people, mental health crises at an all-time high, school shootings, and the list goes on. You can surely add more personal items to the list where you are burdened by unrest, anxious thoughts, fear, and hopelessness. But God is peace. In Him is rest.

One will never find peace in the world. It will not be created by scurrying around and working to ensure everything works as it should. No amount of organization, planning, or hope will create peace. It's not even found when everything is as it should be—oh for a moment maybe, but nothing stays the same, and it won't take long before something comes into the day to disrupt that peace. Peace is not external, based on circumstances; if it were, it would cease to exist before many days.

Peace beyond our understanding is internal, from the Father who sees all, knows all, and will have the final say. It is based on Him, and this Scripture gives us the way to have peace that cannot be stolen away or disrupted: by keeping our minds on the One who is the peace giver.

The Word is full of information about God. He is the Alpha and the Omega, both the Beginning and the End. His thoughts of you are immeasurable, and He knows you. He is our Abba Father, the Master, the Teacher, the Creator, and the Great I AM. There is much to know about the One sitting on the throne. We can spend every minute of our entire lives learning about Him, but that is not enough time. We can know about Him, but we must also know Him. Both are parallel, and both are accomplished simultaneously by reading the Word.

When one's mind stays on the Father, it cannot focus on a trial. If you trust the Father, you know He will take care, in His timing and way, of every anxious thought that comes to you so you can take your eyes off the trouble and put them on the Way-maker.

When trouble comes, our first thought is, "What will I do?" Others will ask the same question. We seem foolish when the answer is "Nothing. I will do nothing but pray and ask the Lord to do what He promised. He will make a way where there seems, in my human mind, to be no way and to provide what I need. However He wishes to do so." Full stop. That is what is required for peace—to trust the One who has the answer.

Be aware of the lies the enemy will try to slip into your mind. He will try to tempt you to take control back, figure it out, and run in circles trying to solve the problem you already know you cannot solve. You will become weary, tired, frustrated, angry, and fearful of trying.

Instead, *submit yourself and your burden to God, resist the devil, and he will flee.* (James 4:7) Then, *the peace of God, which is beyond all understanding, will guard your heart and mind in Christ Jesus* (Philippians 4:7).

WHAT TRUTH DO I NOW KNOW ABOUT GOD?

_____

_____

_____

_____

_____

Is this characteristic of God an internal truth for ME?_____

- Write this characteristic on a sticky note and place it where you'll see it daily. GOD GIVES ME PEACE.

- Read the following verses on God's peace: John 14:27. Romans 5:1. Psalm 119:165.

- On the following page, write down the lies you've been told that have made you doubt God's peace. Use these Scriptures to find the truth: write them down.

MY PRAYER

Father, finding peace in this world is hard. There is none to be found, nothing to put my hope in. But You have told me where to find peace, and here I am, asking for a double portion. Remind me the world has nothing to offer me and that I should instead look to You. Let me walk in so much peace that those around me ask me about it so I can direct them to You.

You never promised that I'd find peace in this world, but You are peace. Help me to stay so near You that I enjoy my days under Your wing. Cause me to rest deeply in You, knowing that You see, know, and walk with me. Father, when I step away from You, out from Your shadow, remind me quickly to move closer to You.

The liar whispers:

_____

_____

_____

_____

BUT GOD SAYS:

_____

_____

_____

_____

_____

_____

_____

_____

_____

_____

_____

_____

_____

HE RENEWS

... but they who wait for the LORD shall renew their strength; they shall mount up with wings like eagles; they shall run and not be weary; they shall walk and not faint.

Isaiah 40:31

Recently, I spotted a bald eagle perched on a post. This rare sight captivated me. I slowed down and observed this majestic creature unfurling its wings and gracefully ascending into the sky. I watched as the eagle's wings made two smooth and powerful motions that carried the eagle high enough until it needed no more effort of its own. Instead, it caught an air current, where it calmly soared on the wind without effort.

For as long as it was in my view, it did not make even one more motion with its wings. Since the wind was carrying it, it had no need to expend energy, so there was no reason it would become tired. Suddenly, this verse made sense.

The enemy would have us wind ourselves up, running in circles with confusion and endless battles, trying to make our plans come to life. The liar entices with, "Do it yourself, look after yourself, take care of yourself." And in so doing, we wear ourselves out.

Just as an eagle needs to rest occasionally, we must also rest. Our lives are filled with busyness. We go to work, record albums, go to the gym, and have fun with our family and friends, among many other things. But there are times when resting is required.

Scripture says that a person plans his ways, but the Lord directs the steps (Proverbs 16:9). This often requires waiting.

But waiting on the Lord is not a passive act. It is an active trust in His timing and His plans. It is a choice to rest in His sovereignty and His goodness even when we don't understand His ways. This kind of waiting is not easy and requires resting, but it is essential for our spiritual growth and ability to soar like an eagle.

Abraham waited for years to hold his promised son. He did not wait well. He scurried around, trying to make it happen, and in so doing, created a mess. On the other hand, we can look at Joseph, who waited with grace. Joseph had ample reason to try and make his own path; he was an innocent man imprisoned. He did interpret a dream and instructed his friend to tell the king of Joseph's skills in hopes of being released. That failed.

But the day did come; God planned for the king to have another dream that disturbed him. Joseph's old friend remembered his dream interpreting skills and told the king, who promptly went to the imprisoned man.

God's timing is impeccable. He is already at the end of the story. We see from the beginning and think we know the way forward, but it is all about us in our planning. With God, it is never just about us. God used Joseph to save Israel from famine. God used Noah to save the human race. God used Moses to free the Israelites, and God will use you for great and mighty things. Rest assured, those things will not be for only your benefit. Who knows how many others He wants to save through you?

The enemy would have you hurry ahead, figure it out, wear out, and faint. But the Lord says, "Wait on Me. I will get you where you are going in My timing, and it will be more than you hoped for. You will not get weary in the process."

WHAT TRUTH DO I NOW KNOW ABOUT GOD?

_____

_____

_____

_____

_____

_____

Is this characteristic of God an internal truth for ME?_____

- Write this characteristic on a sticky note and place it where you'll see it daily. GOD RENEWS ME.

- Read the following verses on how God renews:
  2 Corinthians 5:17, 2 Corinthians 4:16, Lam.3:22-23.

- On the following page, write down the lies you've been told that have made you doubt that God can renew you. Use these Scriptures to find the truth: write them down.

MY PRAYER

God, I am weary. I get tired of trying to make my own plans come to fruition. When I wait on You, I see that You will cause things to work together in Your timing to bring about the desired result. Remind me that You are in my present and future, and You can be trusted to get me where You want me to be.

I surrender my scurrying to You and ask that You give me the grace to wait in peace and rest. Help me learn to be patient in the waiting and not to pout and huff around frustrated, but rejoice to know that Your way is much better than mine.

The liar whispers:

BUT GOD SAYS:

HE IS EVERLASTING

Lift up your eyes on high and see: who created these? He who brings out their host by number, calling them all by name; by the greatness of his might and because he is strong in power, not one is missing ... Have you not known? Have you not heard? The LORD is the everlasting God, the Creator of the ends of the earth. He does not faint or grow weary; his understanding is unsearchable.

Isaiah 40:26, 28

Who is this Mighty One, seated on the Great White Throne of Heaven, above the earth, watching His creation with compassion and power? Who is He who laughs at His enemies and at whose name every knee will bow and even the enemy's tongue will declare, "Yes, He is the Lord."

If you ponder profound questions that are too big for your mind to envelope or understand, take a moment to pause. Breathe deeply. Step away from the busyness of the day, the endless to-do lists, and the worries that tug at your heart. Sit outside for a time and simply look around. Our Savior can be found.

Everywhere you turn, there is abundant evidence where the peaceful fingerprints of the Master Creator can easily be recognized. The magnificence of His creation is so vast that no one can understand it, even while being nestled right in the middle.

The liar would have you believe there is no God, that the Scriptures are mere stories that sound nice and give the human some sort of crutch to get by in this world. He whispers that we are only the result of some chaotic explosion of energy, drifting aimlessly through life, merely waiting for the ground to reclaim us in death.

The liar's words seek to convince you that if you do not take care of yourself, no one else will. Yet, the deceiver's lies are but a vapor; all it takes to embrace the truth is to open your eyes and truly see what is right in front of you.

Observe the birds of the air flitting joyfully from branch to branch, reveling in the freedom of knowing they are seen and cherished by God. They carry no burdens or anxieties. He knows them. Pause for a moment to watch the rippling waters of a stream, forging their path with grace, unaware of their destination yet trusting in the journey. The Lord directs its path.

Lay back in the cool summer grass, allowing the bright sun to warm your face. Peace is waiting to be realized, woven into every fabric of the Master's creation. If one takes a moment to truly look, the existence of a good God becomes undeniable. We are enveloped by His creation, His peace, and His presence if only we take the time to slow down and look.

Gaze up at the stars, each a testament to the One who delights in you. He calls each star by name, knowing them intimately, and not a single one escapes His sight. If He takes such care to know the stars, which will fade with time and eventually fall from their place in the sky, how much more does He cherish you who will be with Him for eternity?

There is peace in recognizing that this Everlasting God never tires. He never grows weary of our cries for help, pleas for mercy, or broken requests for forgiveness. He crafted all the beauty of this magnificent earth and declared, "It is good."

If He looks upon the transient wonders of the earth and calls them good, how much more does He inhale your uniqueness—an eternal being, who He perfectly and wonderfully created—and says, "You are mine." How much more will He care for you?

You are His greatest joy, prized possession, and most cherished masterpiece. In the quiet moments of reflection, remember that you are loved beyond measure, surrounded by the beauty of creation, and cradled in the arms of a God who delights in every detail of your existence. You are not just a part of His exquisite creation; you are His child in whom He delights.

WHAT TRUTH DO I NOW KNOW ABOUT GOD?

_____

_____

_____

_____

_____

_____

Is this characteristic of God an internal truth for ME?_____

- Write this characteristic on a sticky note and place it where you'll see it daily. GOD IS EVERLASTING.

- Read the following verses on God is everlasting: 1 Timothy 1:17, Psalm 119:89, Revelation 1:8.

- On the following page, write down the lies you've been told that have made you question God's existence. Use these Scriptures to find the truth: write them down.

MY PRAYER

You are the King! You have no beginning and no end. You are the Alpha and Omega, and You created everything with the breath of Your words. Father, how great and mighty You are, and for reasons I cannot understand, You delight in me. This is overwhelming to me that You would choose me to belong to You.

The waves and the wind obey Your voice, the eagles fly where You direct, and a star is never missing because You know where each one is. You have named them and understand them. How much more do You know me, Father? Thank you! Draw me closer to You, fill me with wonder, and help me to walk worthy of the calling You have given to me.

The liar whispers:

BUT GOD SAYS:

HE IS TRUTH

For though we walk in the flesh, we are not waging war according to the flesh. For the weapons of our warfare are not of the flesh but have divine power to destroy strongholds. We destroy arguments and every lofty opinion raised against the knowledge of God, and take every thought captive to obey Christ ...

2 Corinthians 10:3-5

The enemy plays dirty. He does not wage war where we can see it, but instead, slinks into our minds where he thinks his tactics are hidden from our understanding. The mind is a battleground. It is where the enemy plants seeds of doubt and threads of lies meant to tangle and ensnare us. It can be exhausting; battles always are. Being unable to distance ourselves from our minds sets up a wild game of cat and mouse. We can't opt out or pass on our turn.

Every day, a new battle threatens to assault us if we don't get ahead of it and defeat the enemy right at the start. The longer we dwell on his lies, the more lies he piles on until we are bent low under the heavy weight of what is not even true. It can wear us down and tempt us to give up. But don't. Instead, learn how to play the game. The Master gave us the weapons we need, and with the power of truth, we can begin to battle less and rest more. Everyone plays this game; you are not alone.

Imagine every thought that comes into your mind as a soldier. They slither in unannounced, skulking around and dropping nuggets. Each pushes through the gate and, without announcing its arrival, bursts into a wild explosion in your mind, and there it is—a thought. Now, think about what you're thinking about! The thoughts do not need your permission to enter the battlefield. But once there, it is your move. What will you do? Keep the thought and empower it by dwelling on it? Or silence it by drowning it in truth and forcing it out?

Only you can decide.

While the choice belongs to you, the Bible directs us toward what should be our move in one step: Take them captive. Take captive every thought the enemy has planted, every single one. Remember, it's a battle. If you let one slip through, it will bring his friends and cause significant damage.

What are some of these thoughts? Thoughts that attack your character sound like this: "You are stupid ... You are a burden ... Nobody likes you ... You are alone ... You're a failure." Or thoughts of temptation sound like this: "It's perfectly fine if you cheat on your test ... It doesn't matter ... Nobody's going to notice if you steal the shoes ... It's a big store, they can afford it ... Just lie ... It's not a big deal... Nobody will ever know, and you won't get in trouble."

These are first-level bottom-feeder thoughts of the enemy. They are lies that attack every person from time to time. They can get much more vile and hurtful, even suggesting violence to yourself or others.

Then, that evil liar tries to insert next-level assaults and make you question if they are actually your own thoughts! "If these are my thoughts, I must be sick or crazy!" Many mental health struggles start in our minds as a thought that was left to fester and grow. If not captivated and kicked out, that thought can run amuck, causing us to doubt everything we know to be true.

You are neither sick nor crazy. You are a strong and capable individual, and you have the power to change the game once you know how to play it. You have the power to stop the thoughts and win not only the battle but the war; win the game! You can be the victor! It gets easier the more you do it, so start today and be vigilant. Think about what you're thinking about. If a thought pops in that contradicts what God says, it is not from Him. Kick it out. Speak God's Word and defeat that thought before it defeats you. Do this repeatedly, and soon, you will find that lying thoughts are less and less. Your mind will be at peace, and you will have won the battle.

WHAT TRUTH DO I NOW KNOW ABOUT GOD?

Is this characteristic of God an internal truth for ME?_____

- Write this characteristic on a sticky note and place it where you'll see it daily. <u>GOD IS THE TRUTH</u>.

- Read the following verses on God's truth: John 8:32, Psalm 119:160, Proverbs 30:5.

- On the following page, write down the lies you've been told that have made you doubt the validity of the Bible. Use these Scriptures to find the truth: write them down.

MY PRAYER

Father, thank you for giving me the tools to win the battles in my mind. I am sure there are battles I fight that are unnecessary simply because I have allowed wrong thoughts to grow roots. Lord, open my understanding to show me what lies I have been believing and give me wisdom and courage to uproot them and toss them out.

Help me to find the truth in Your Word, to combat the lies, and gain victory. Teach me to think about what I'm thinking about and the wisdom to know which thoughts to keep and which to dismiss, and Lord, teach me more of Your truth.

The liar whispers:

_____

_____

_____

_____

BUT GOD SAYS:

_____

_____

_____

_____

_____

_____

_____

_____

_____

_____

_____

_____

_____

_____

www.ingramcontent.com/pod-product-compliance
Lightning Source LLC
Jackson TN
JSHW070725210125
77401JS00003B/4